BRIGHT N

THE BROTHERS KARAMAZOV BY FYODOR DOSTOYEVSKY

Intelligent Education

INFLUENCE
PUBLISHERS

Nashville, Tennessee

BRIGHT NOTES: The Brothers Karamazov
www.BrightNotes.com

No part of this publication may be used or reproduced in any manner whatsoever without written permission, except in the case of brief quotations in critical articles and reviews. For permissions, contact Influence Publishers http://www.influencepublishers.com.

ISBN: 978-1-645421-40-5 (Paperback)
ISBN: 978-1-645421-41-2 (eBook)

Published in accordance with the U.S. Copyright Office Orphan Works and Mass Digitization report of the register of copyrights, June 2015.

Originally published by Monarch Press.
H. Richmond Neuville; John D. Simons; Ursula Simons, 1965
2020 Edition published by Influence Publishers.

Interior design by Lapiz Digital Services. Cover Design by Thinkpen Designs.

Printed in the United States of America.

Library of Congress Cataloging-in-Publication Data forthcoming.
Names: Intelligent Education
Title: BRIGHT NOTES: The Brothers Karamazov
Subject: STU004000 STUDY AIDS / Book Notes

CONTENTS

FYODOR DOSTOYEVKSY

. . . .

Biographical Sketch of Dostoyevsky

Fyodor Mikhailovich Dostoyevsky was born October 30, 1821 in Moscow, the second son of Mikhail, a physician at the Maryinski Hospital for the Poor. The family belonged to the hereditary nobility and possessed a small country estate worked by some one hundred "souls" as serfs were then called. Late every spring the family left Moscow to spend the summer there.

After Fyodor completed his secondary education, his father sent him in 1838 to St. Petersburg where he entered the College of Engineers, a military school run by the Czar. Although he studied hard and in general made a good impression on his teachers, the young cadet was in constant financial straits. Always writing home for more money, he describes his "terrible plight" in the most urgent terms. When money came, though, he celebrated its arrival with a huge banquet and drinking party for his friends, or gambled it away shooting pool. He was generous to the point of self-destruction. When his brother Mikhail was married, Fyodor sent him one hundred fifty rubles. Two weeks later he was broke again, begging him for five. This inability to manage his finances persisted throughout his life. In fact, he was nearly always on the brink of bankruptcy.

Despite his ups and downs in Petersburg, the twenty-three-year-old Dostoyevsky became so attached to the city that the mere thought of living elsewhere was unbearable for him. So when he learned that he was about to be posted to the provinces, he resigned his commission and resolved to support himself by writing. In 1846 *Poor Folk* was published and immediately became a best seller. The young author was lionized as the new Gogol, received into the best houses, and became the object of unrestrained praise. The novel is a brilliantly written though sentimental story about the destructive effects of poverty. In quick succession there followed *The Double* (1846) and a collection of short stories under the title *White Nights* (1848).

About this time Dostoyevsky became seriously ill, both mentally and physically. Poor, quarrelsome, the victim of unpredictable fevers and convulsions, he soon alienated his admirers as well as his editors. Furthermore, since his erratic behavior was put down to personality rather than to the illness that it was, he was frequently laughed at, jeered, and mocked. Turgenev, for instance, so despised him that he would engage him in conversation merely for the pleasure of torturing him. Still, Dostoyevsky was reckoned among the most promising young writers of the day. Unfortunately, his literary career was suddenly interrupted by a remarkable incident that was the direct consequence of his political involvement.

Sentenced To Death

Ever since the Decembrist revolt in 1825 it had become fashionable for men of learning to promote social reform.

Revolutionary manifestoes were printed abroad, smuggled into the country, and widely distributed. Czar Nicholas I, however, was determined that there would be no revolution in Russia under him. Censorship was severe and many domestic and foreign authors were banned. The penalties for revolutionary activity were increased, and government spies were everywhere. Notwithstanding, Dostoyevsky joined a group of political rebels who met every Friday evening at Mikhail Petrashevsky's apartment. Here they discussed different political trends, plotting revolution on the side in a rather harmless way. All the same, the government became suspicious. The members of the circle were arrested, brought to trial, and Dostoyevsky, along with several others, was sentenced to death.

Finally, on a cold winter morning after a miserable stay in prison, the future author and his co-conspirators were driven to their place of execution. There, tied to stakes, the unlucky men faced the firing squad. However, as the soldiers were given the order to aim, a horseman suddenly appeared riding full tilt across the square. He bore a letter from the Czar commuting all the death sentences to prison terms. The entire affair was prearranged to frighten them and others of their kind into submission to the Czarist regime.

"To Live, No Matter How"

Needless to say, Dostoyevsky was profoundly affected by this brief encounter with death. So much so in fact that the **theme** of the condemned man appears on countless occasions in his letters, articles, and novels. Among the most forceful passages describing the condemned man's state of mind occurs in *Crime and Punishment* when Raskolnikov says: "Someone condemned to death thinks an hour before his death that if he had to live on a steep pinnacle or on a rock or on a cliff edge so narrow that there was only room to stand, and around him there were abysses, the ocean, and everlasting darkness, eternal solitude, eternal tempests - if he had to remain standing on a few square inches of space for a thousand years or all eternity, it would be better to live than to die. Only to live, to live, to live, no matter how."

Dostoyevsky's will to live was severely tested by the Czar's verdict. He was sentenced to four years' hard labor in Siberia followed by another five as a common soldier in a penal battalion. The years of physical hardship, loneliness, and the study of the Bible, the only reading allowed the prisoners, completely changed the author's way of thinking. In both religion and politics he turns into an outspoken conservative, a staunch supporter of the Czarist regime, and the Russian Orthodox Church. He becomes convinced that an Orthodox Christian will, of his own accord, subject himself joyfully to the will of God. Furthermore, by some mystic fiat, a true Russian's political strivings will miraculously coincide with the will of the Czar Emancipator. These attitudes form the basis of Dostoyevsky's dialectical thought and ultimately determine whether his heroes are saved or destroyed.

Thus when in 1859, ten years after his arrest, Dostoyevsky is permitted to resign from the army and return to Petersburg, we meet a changed writer, but not a less productive one. Shortly after his release he publishes an account of his imprisonment, *Notes from the House of the Dead* (1860). This is followed by the short novel *The Insulted and the Injured* (1861). He even tries his hand at journalism, successfully editing his own paper. Unfortunately, his troubles with the regime are not over. His journal, *Vremya*, is considered subversive and ordered closed. Disgusted, Dostoyevsky decides to leave Russia for Europe.

In Wiesbaden he won a large sum of money which allowed him the luxury of an affair with the beautiful, charming, and intelligent Polina Suslova. They toured Europe together visiting all the "in" places until he lost his money. Possessing a destructive passion for gambling, he could not keep away from the casinos. On several occasions he lost everything and had to write friends in Russia for the fare home.

The novel *The Gambler* (1866) is a thinly veiled autobiographical account of this trip. The book is also the third major work in the most productive period of his life which begins in 1864 with the publication of *Notes from Underground*. During the next sixteen years Dostoyevsky worked feverishly, producing among other things five major novels and *The Diary of a Writer*. In addition, he maintained a voluminous correspondence with friends, acquaintances, and various admirers who wrote for advice.

Marriage And Fame

Dostoyevsky's existence changed for the better with his marriage to Anna Snitkina, his secretary. Among her many qualities was a good business sense that enabled her to offset her husband's inability to manage his finances. There were trips abroad and every summer the family rented a small cottage in the country. Dostoyevsky could now truly enjoy his fame as one of Russia's leading authors and was finally able to write at his leisure.

Yet Dostoyevsky's health was always bad. Since his return from Siberia he suffered from epilepsy and these attacks increased with alarming frequency in the 1860s. During the worst period the fits came once a month and so exhausted him that he needed several days to recover. In addition, he contracted tuberculosis in the 1870s which, together with lung cancer, precipitated his death January 28, 1881.

St. Petersburg: Dostoyevsky's Bad Dream

The background of many of the author's stories, Dostoyevsky's St. Petersburg seems to be a flat, featureless wasteland. Its buildings lack character and its streets are dismal alleyways rarely touched by daylight. To Dostoyevsky, St. Petersburg seemed often so unreal that he was haunted by the prospect that it was simply someone's dream and that upon awakening everything would disappear leaving only the marshes and lakes. Others had felt likewise before him. When Peter the Great realized his ambition to build a city upon the Finnish marsh, the peasants living in the vicinity thought that it had been pulled down from the sky. It is only fitting that in such a city human activity is subdued. There is no hustle and bustle in Dostoyevsky's city streets, nor do we find the comforting noise of people going about their daily business. Rarely anything takes place in open daylight. The city seems to be condemned to perpetual twilight through which Dostoyevsky's characters hurry to their non-descript lodgings.

Thus, Dostoyevsky never describes a city in the manner of Balzac. In fact, he had an antipathy toward any kind of description of buildings or landscapes, saying that he had better things to do than waste time over creating word pictures. Consequently, he draws the barest outlines and leaves the reader to fill in the details. From another angle, this method is all the more effective because it allows the reader to create his own image of the city.

We could say that the author conceives St. Petersburg like a map. He chooses a location and then strictly adheres to its dimensions. In *Crime and Punishment*, for example, we know exactly where Raskolnikov lives, how many paces to the moneylender's house, and how far it is to the police station. Often Dostoyevsky's favorite places are the ones he personally knows. Central to *Crime and Punishment* is Haymarket Square close to which the author lived for many years. An unbelievably filthy quarter, it is the gathering place of thieves, prostitutes and the like. Surrounding the square are the stalls from which are hawked all manner of merchandise of use only to the destitute. Leading off the square are trash-filled alleyways bordered by pothouses and bodakings of the worst kind. Like Raskolnikov, Dostoyevsky loved to wander aimlessly about the place filling his lungs with the fetid air as if he were inhaling the essence of being. Still, precise descriptions of the place are absent. The scenery resembles a rather hastily erected stage set. Yet, we sense it as real because the characters are real, often uncomfortably so.

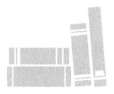

THE BROTHERS KARAMAZOV

This is the last and the greatest of his novels and one of the most powerful works in world literature. Properly speaking, it is not a novel at all, but a panorama of the human soul in relation to the forces and problems that have afflicted the human mind from classical antiquity to the present day.

Of the four central characters, the three brothers and their father each represents a particular philosophy of life. The father, Fyodor, worships the senses with little concern for anything else. Many readers see him as Dostoyevsky's self-portrait. This is true only if we see in all the main characters different aspects of the author's self.

Ivan, his first born, is his exact opposite. An enlightened rationalist, he insists that his way of life is determined solely by reason. A religious skeptic, he is tortured by the question: "If there is really no God, then is everything permissible?" Believing Ivan's arguments, his half-brother Smerdyakov murders Fyodor. In this way Ivan and his "idea" become responsible for his father's death and Smerdyakov's consequent suicide.

The second brother, Alyosha, personifies the principle of Christianity at its best, the love of one's neighbor and of all creation. Dmitri, the third brother, embodies Russia's primitive spirit. Driven by instincts he swirls through the novel like a demonic force.

The Brothers Karamazov is concerned above all with man's search for meaning and his battle with doubt and alienation. The characters believe that beyond or within the phenomenal world there exists an ultimate reality. In their struggle for faith they hurtle against one another with destructive force, creating suffering and despair. Fatally addicted to crime, driven by lusts and passions of every kind, they are kept from their goal by the very intensity of their search.

THE BROTHERS KARAMAZOV

TEXTUAL ANALYSIS

PART ONE

· ·

BOOK I

Introduction

The **theme** of the novel is man's search for God. In this quest each of the three brothers represents a major aspect of man's existence. The eldest brother, Dmitri, embodies man's physical nature. He is said to possess the "Karamazov spirit," which means that like his father he has an unbridled, mercurial nature and values sensual experiences as well as material possessions. The second brother, Ivan, represents man's intellectual capacities. He rejects God's existence as inconsistent with reason and feels justified in saying: "If there is no God, then everything is lawful." Alyosha, the third and youngest of the brothers, signifies man's desire to transcend his earthly existence. He believes in God and Christ and in the possibility of bringing the kingdom of Heaven to earth through charity and the love of one's neighbor. Although each brother represents one aspect of human existence, they are not pure symbols because each feels and responds to the influence of the other two.

Fyodor Pavlovitch

The greater part of Book I is devoted to Fyodor Pavlovitch and to the circumstances that bring the family together. Dostoyevsky gives a particularly vivid description of the old man's face. It is repulsive in every aspect. He has bloated features, suspicious little eyes swimming in fat, and an unnaturally large Adam's apple that describes an arc from his chin to his neck. Not only is his mouth filled with the stubby remains of decayed teeth, he has a tendency to slobber as well.

Fyodor's physical repulsiveness is exceeded only by his moral degradation. Between orgies, the old man devotes his time to amassing wealth in dubious enterprises, usually at the expense of others. Nor does he have any sense of responsibility. When his first wife runs away in disgust with a divinity student leaving him with a small child, Fyodor enthusiastically takes up drinking and debauchery. He completely forgets about his son Dmitri who is left to be raised by the family serfs. His second marriage to a sixteen-year-old girl is provoked more by lust than from any feeling of love. His callousness, degraded life style, and almost total indifference to common decency soon precipitate her death. But not before she bears him two sons, Ivan and Alyosha, who would have fared no better than Dmitri had not the mother's family taken them away to be raised in a distant province. What circumstances could bring such a family together?

Dmitri has come to town on business. Believing that his mother left him a small estate and sensing moreover that his father means to cheat him of it, he realizes that he must take immediate action if he is to get anything at all. Ivan's presence remains a mystery for most of the book, but we eventually discover that he has followed the woman he loves, Katerina Ivanovna. She in turn, has followed the person she loves, Dmitri. Alyosha's visit, by contrast, has no selfish purpose. He merely wants to see his mother's grave. He soon comes into contact with the famous elder Zossima, and when the novel begins he has decided to become a monk under the elder's guidance.

Alyosha As Christ Figure

Shortly before beginning work on *The Idiot*, Dostoyevsky asked in a letter whether it would be possible to create a **protagonist** based on the character of Christ without the result appearing sentimental or ridiculous. How would He impress us if He were suddenly sent to earth stripped of His divinity and mission and told to get along as best He could? What would He be like? How would He interact with others? And most important, could He survive in nineteenth century Russia? This **theme** is most intensely dramatized in the figure of Prince Myshkin, the hero of *The Idiot*. Ultimately, Dostoyevsky was dissatisfied with Prince Myshkin because at the end he is overwhelmed by forces he can neither understand nor control. In Alyosha, Dostoyevsky finally succeeds in creating a believable hero based on the ideal of Christ.

We learn that like Christ, Alyosha lives in the ordinary world but in a way is not a part of it. He is aware of traditional material values and social behavior, but he is indifferent to them. The spiritual strength of Alyosha puts him beyond good and evil. Thus he refuses to make value judgments, accepts people as they are, and believes in the inherent good of mankind. And finally, he sees himself as endlessly and hopelessly more sinful than others.

Spirit Of The Karamazovs

Before continuing with the analysis, we must define what is meant by "the spirit of the Karamazovs," a term that occurs throughout the novel. On the most superficial level it appears as a crude, earthly force that puts sensual pleasure above everything. The spirit seems to rise from the realm of untamed instincts and in its worst forms, has an element of savagery. Fyodor has completely abandoned himself to its pull and it frequently threatens to engulf all the brothers. But the "spirit" has another side. On a higher level it involves a unique way of looking at life.

The Karamazovs tend to make little distinction between "good" and "bad." Regarding everything as relative, they see divinity and nobility even in criminal acts. In contrast to traditional morality which formalizes rules into an ethical code, they regard all conflicting elements as parts of a greater whole. We may better understand this idea through the following example.

Suppose that a person is confronted by two equally valid facts, X and Y, but he is asked to make a moral distinction between the two anyway. If he is like most men, he will make a decision based on his past experiences and if they tell him that X is good and Y is bad he will codify them as such. Furthermore, he believes in a god who approves of X and rejects Y. The Karamazovs on the other hand, worship a deity who represents both X and Y. Thus the god of the Karamazovs does not acknowledge polarities because he is able to view existence from a perspective that both transcends and affirms all of them.

This way of looking at things stands out in sharp relief to the modern mind which interprets the world as consisting of such opposites as illusion and reality, good and evil, duty and inclination, spirit and flesh, love and hate. The list could be endlessly multiplied. Such opposites have been created in an effort to render the world comprehensible. In this novel, Dostoyevsky claims they are illusions. In fact, he seems to say that it is quite possible that opposites are identical and that the value of one extreme lies in its identity with its polar opposite. Creation and destruction, for example, could be considered manifestations of the same creative process.

Any person who understands, even for an instant, the interchangeability of good and evil, the relativity of all values, becomes automatically the enemy of structured society because civilization as we know it depends upon the existence of prohibition as well as of affirmation. Dmitri, Ivan, Alyosha, Zossima all experience in different ways the reversibility of concepts. To think in this way can lead to despair as in Ivan's case, or to a spiritual reevaluation as it is with Dmitri and Alyosha who begin to see chaos as the normal scheme of things. They realize that to create a new order, with new values, a person must leave this society and start from the beginning. For the Karamazovs, destruction is looked upon as a positive value for it precedes creation.

Elders

Chapter Five of Book I introduces the elder Zossima. As Dostoyevsky describes him, Zossima is distinguished by two qualities: his self-knowledge and his courage to be himself. Through self-mastery he has gained almost absolute freedom from society and its value systems as well as from his instincts. He attained self-knowledge by forcing himself to look into the debts of his self and accept what he finds there. He has admitted to himself that besides all his noble qualities, he, like other men, is also prejudiced, vindictive, petty, and quite often disposed to violence and sensuality. But unlike most other men, he does not regard these aspects of his self as evil but as integral parts of his personality. Zossima teaches that the unnatural repression of one's impulses is harmful. In terms of modern psychology, what Zossima is saying is that if these primal urges are exposed to the light of day they can be reassimilated by the personality and given a constructive form. Worst of all, he will say in the next chapter, it would be wrong for a person to regard himself as evil when he senses these forces within himself. We can illustrate the elder's ideas with a hypothetical situation:

Suppose that I desire the death of my father for some reason. Since society calls this the greatest evil, I will, if I am like most people, automatically look upon myself as an evil person for having such thoughts at all. Even the New Testament does not distinguish between the thought and the deed. The facts of the matter, however, are different. Both psychologists and theologians point out time and again that such thoughts do occur and that they are common. The danger to my psyche occurs when I conclude that I am basically evil or unnatural for wishing my father's death. Zossima, too, says that we should ignore the social tradition that teaches us to repress our impulses. Rather we must peer into the depths of our "selves" and confront the primordial urges we find there and use our will to act or not to act upon them.

We now understand what Zossima means when he says that self-knowledge is of primary importance, because in knowing oneself the individual then knows and understands all mankind. The dictum "tout comprendre c'est tout pardoner" (to understand all is to forgive all) suddenly takes on profound significance. People come to Zossima to confess, to seek advice, and to ask his blessing because they know that he understands them and will not pass judgment.

On the surface "the spirit of the Karamazovs" and Zossima's digression from social and theological standards may appear to sanction crime. Dostoyevsky's heroes are not willful criminals. Stopping short of the actual deed, they are satisfied to think about crime, and to acknowledge the potentiality within themselves.

BOOK II

Theme

The action of Book II takes place within the monastery. The Karamazov family has gathered in the cell of Father Zossima so that he may decide Dmitri's and Fyodor's dispute about the inheritance. At first unwilling to assume the role of judge, Zossima reluctantly yields to his superiors who think that his mediation could benefit the institution. Fyodor had already donated a thousand rubles to the memory of his second wife and might give more while the other guest, Miusov, might be persuaded to drop his lawsuit against the monastery over timber and fishing rights. This, in brief, is the episode's outer framework which takes second place to Dostoyevsky's real interest: to show Zossima at work.

Zossima is a holy man. For years thousands of people have come to him, sometimes traveling hundreds of miles just to confess and receive his blessing. For the most part, these supplicants are in great despair. Their problems are many. Unresolved guilt feelings seem to predominate. Although Zossima is terribly exhausted and knows he will soon die, he continues to receive visitors in the courtyard because he has an immense compassion for the afflicted.

Rumors to the contrary, Zossima does not perform miracles. But he does have a marvelous talent which enables him to see a person for what he really is, quite often to that own person's surprise. Add to this genuine concern, understanding and love, and we know why the supplicants benefit from their visit to him. For instance, a woman who was mistreated by her husband suddenly realized at his funeral how glad she was about his death and what a misfortune it would be if he suddenly returned to life. A simple peasant, she was terrified by this thought, regarding herself as inherently evil and thus unworthy of God's forgiveness. But Zossima tells her that under the circumstances the thought was understandable. The important thing is not the thought itself, but rather her attitude toward it: "Be not angry if you are wronged. Forgive the dead man what wrong he did to you. Be reconciled with him in truth. If you are penitent, you love, and if you love you are of God. All things are atoned for, all things are saved by love. If I, a sinner, even as you are, am tender with you and have pity on you, how much more will God. Love is such a priceless treasure that you can redeem the whole world by it, and expiate not only your own sins but the sins of others."

This quotation underscores the importance Zossima places upon love. For him, and for Dostoyevsky who is speaking through him, love has the power to abolish the sufferings of all mankind. By love he does not mean the affection shared by members of the same family, or the delirium of a youthful romance, but simply a genuine regard for people and concern for their welfare. Zossima is careful to point out, however, that respect for others is impossible unless we respect ourselves. This is why he warns Mme. Hohlakov and the other women there not to fear what they find out about themselves. Should they suddenly discover some appalling side of their nature that does not coincide with their self-image, they should not try to deny its existence. To do so is not only an act of self-rejection but also one of self-deception. Deceitfulness towards oneself leads to dishonesty toward others and finally culminates in self-hate which then abolishes any possibility of love: "Above all, avoid falsehood," he says in Chapter 4, "especially falsehood to yourself.... What seems to you bad within you will grow purer from the very fact of your observing it in yourself. Avoid fear, too, though fear is the only consequence of every sort of falsehood."

In Chapters 3 and 4 Zossima demonstrates Dostoyevsky's ideas about Christianity and its role in men's lives. The author believes that the Christian doctrine of brotherly love, kindness, and charity is the only valid system of values that will ultimately save mankind from itself. But he lived in a century when Christianity had become suspect, incapable of dealing with the problems of an increasingly complex society. He was keenly aware that the socialists and intelligentsia of the period advocated various rational schemes of social organization that were designed to replace the function of the church in bringing happiness to mankind. Dostoyevsky violently disagreed with these utopians, pointing out that the weakness of their theories lay precisely in their rationality. He sees man as a composite of rational and irrational elements and maintains that any philosophy of life that does not take this into account is doomed to fail.

In part, Dostoyevsky wrote *The Brothers Karamazov* to test two different approaches to solving mankind's spiritual and social problems. His own personal view, represented by Alyosha and Zossima, is basically Christian and stresses individual freedom and brotherly love. By contrast, the reformers, represented by Ivan, call for the establishment of a kind of Christian totalitarianism that denies the value of freedom and love. Instead, the church will use spiritual coercion to bring about social harmony. Even though the novel ends in favor of Dostoyevsky's special kind of Christianity, it is not because he has stacked the deck. On the contrary, logic and reason are almost always on the side of the opponents and they have the Grand Inquisitor as their most articulate spokesman. In Chapter Six the first of many debates on the subject takes place.

Ivan's Article

The discussion in Chapter Six revolves about Ivan's review of the book *On the Foundations of Church Jurisdiction*. The discussion is soon enlarged to include the concept of crime and divine punishment. Ivan claims that if crime is to be permanently erased, then the Church must absorb the State. A new deterrent could then be erected before the potential criminal: excommunication. Through this device the criminal would be cut off not only from men but also from the Church.

To everyone's surprise, Zossima points out that the Church already acts as a deterrent and that it is unnecessary and in a way unethical to bring about a fusing of Church and State laws. Unlike Ivan, Zossima stresses not excommunication as a deterrent but the pain of individual conscience: ".... the real punishment, the only effectual one, the only deterrent and softening one ... lies in the recognition of sin by conscience." Here the basic difference between these views is clear. Ivan sees the function of the Church in purely practical terms: how can it be used to prevent crime? Ultimately, his ideas culminate in the absolutism of the Grand

Inquisitor. Zossima, on the other hand, knows that to employ excommunication as punishment would mean to reject the whole mission of Christianity which is not to exercise control but to help: "The Church does not excommunicate him but simply persists in fatherly exhortation of him ... and there must be at least some one to have pity on him."

No Morality Without Immortality

Closely connected to these ideas is Ivan's insight that belief in immortality is the basis of all morality. He points out that there is no natural law stipulating that man should love his neighbor or **refrain** from crime. According to him, man needs an incentive to be moral. He thinks that since dying is terrifying, the promise of everlasting life as reward for moral excellence exercises the most powerful influence on a Christian life. If this belief is taken away, man will revert to his primitive instincts. Crimes then become inevitable and are indeed a logical outcome of Ivan's position.

The brief exchange about this idea contains Zossima's astonishing insight that Ivan believes neither in immortality nor in what he has written in his article on Church jurisdiction. He is a desperate man who wants to believe and suffers immensely because he is unable to. It is ironic that the source of Ivan's despair arises from his self-deception, precisely what Zossima warned the peasant women about.

The Scandalous Scene

Even before arriving at the elder's, Fyodor had decided to play the buffoon and make a fool of himself so as to outrage everyone who might be present. First, he needles the pseudo-intellectual

Miusov; then when Dmitri arrives he works himself into an artificial rage so that his insults will sound convincing. Fyodor's absurd behavior, the shouting and screaming soon bring to the surface Dmitri's intense hatred of his father. When Zossima realizes that this hatred is strong enough to lead to murder, he gets up, walks over to Dmitri, and bows to him, touching the floor with his forehead in the Russian fashion. This act remains a mystery to everyone. Later we learn that this was the elder's way of showing sympathy for the immense suffering in store for Dmitri.

This scene has only a momentarily calming effect on the party. Once outside and then later at the luncheon the yelling and insults reach their former intensity until finally the group breaks up in a tragic-comic hullabaloo.

BOOK III

Theme

Book III provides a closer look at Dmitri. In Chapters Three, Four, and Five called "Confessions of a Passionate Heart" Dmitri recounts how the Karamazov spirit is corrupting his life and turning him into an "insect." He begins by quoting from Schiller's "Das Eleusische Fest," a poem of particular significance because he thinks it accurately defines his position within the world. In the poem Ceres descends from Mt. Olympus in search of her daughter Proserpine and is appalled by what she finds. War ravages the land and "where'er the grieving goddess/ Turns her melancholy gaze,/ Sunk in vilest degradation/ Man his loathsomeness displays." Here Dmitri breaks into tears because he sees this degradation in himself. Yet it is not the existence of vileness that distresses Dmitri but his fondness of it. One side of him positively exults in vice and cruelty, in seeking out adventures in what he calls the "moral back alleys behind the main road." He even prides himself on the thoroughness of his debauchery. And what is still more awesome is that he finds a kind of beauty there, the beauty of Sodom. Here Dostoyevsky illuminates one of the great mysteries of the human condition; the fact that a man can pursue everything that is just, refined, and noble - "The Ideal of the Madonna" - and at the same time love everything that is savage, base, and vile - "the ideal of Sodom." "Yes, man is broad, too broad," he declaims in Chapter Three. "I'd have him narrower. The devil only knows what to make of it. What to the mind is shameful is beauty and nothing else to the heart. Is there beauty in Sodom? Believe me, that for the immense mass of mankind beauty is found in Sodom." Dostoyevsky believes that man is able to combine within himself all possible opposites. As a representative of mankind, Dmitri is a vessel of contradictions.

For example, Dmitri tells Alyosha a story about how on a midnight sleigh ride he took liberties with his date, a young girl whom he was with for the first time. Then instead of making her an offer of marriage the next day, as customs prevailing at that time dictated, he ignored her. At dances he watched her out of the corner of his eye, enjoying her indignation. "This game only tickled that insect lust I cherished in my soul."

But even in the light of this and Dmitri's other equally base stories, he has both the author's and the reader's sympathy because, unlike Fyodor who is a hopeless case, Dmitri never loses sight of the ideal. In fact, he is horrified by this moral breadth, this unlimited capacity for good and bad. This is crucial for Dostoyevsky. The unforgiveable sin in Dostoyevsky's world is indifference. Svidrigaylov in *Crime and Punishment*, Stavrogin in *The Possessed*, and Fyodor in this novel are all doomed from the outset because of their indifference to evil. Dostoyevsky does not condemn these protagonists because there is an evil dimension to them, but because they have lost sight of the ideal and have become morally stagnant. The important factor in matters of the author's ethical judgment is that man never reach that position in which he can no longer distinguish between good and evil. Dmitri is saved at the end of the novel because he regrets his transgressions and seeks to atone for them, after a fashion. Thus after exploring the young girl's body in the sleigh, he never says a word to anyone about it so as not to ruin her reputation. There are other occasions when Dmitri shows that he has not lost sight of the good, as for instance in his efforts to pay back the money he owes his fiancé Katerina.

Confession Of A Passionate Heart

The story of Dmitri's involvement with Katerina illuminates the spirit of the Karamazovs at work from a different angle. The reader perceives immediately that even though the two are betrothed, marriage would be a **catastrophe** for both because from the outset their relationship is poisoned by a desire for mutual revenge. In the beginning, Dmitri merely wants to play her a caddish trick for treating him haughtily at a dance. One day he hears that her father, the divisional commander, is in serious trouble because he cannot repay 4500 rubles that he took from the divisional cash box. Seeing his chance for revenge, Dmitri sends word to Katerina that he is willing to pay 4500 for her body. When she finally visits him to save her father's reputation, Dmitri quickly sees that if he is to "win the game" and humiliate her, his actions must exceed hers in nobility, his sacrifice must be greater than hers. So he gives her the money, opens the door, and bows to her. Her return bow to Dmitri, however, is more than an act of gratitude, it is one of self-punishment. For she has been forced to take money from someone whom she despises without any notion of when she can pay it back, if ever. Moreover, she is now morally in his debt and the remainder of her life will be an effort to pay it back by making an equally great sacrifice: herself.

The letter Katerina writes to Dmitri shows how she envisions their future life together: "I love you madly even if you don't love me, never mind. Be my husband. Don't be afraid. I won't hamper you in any way. I will be your chattel, I will be the carpet under your feet. I want to love you forever. I want to save you from yourself." In other words, she wants to be dishonored, mistreated, and humiliated in order to pay her debt in the noblest fashion. Small wonder that Dmitri wants to break the engagement. He knows that she does not love him but only imagines it: "She loves her own virtue, not me."

Three Thousand Rubles

The symbol of this polluted relationship is the three thousand rubles Dmitri owes Katerina. It becomes one of the most important factors in the development of the novel. She gives him the money to send to one of her relatives. But before he gets to the post office he meets Grushenka, falls in love with her, and they spend half of it on a three-day orgy. (Dmitri tells everyone that they spent it all.) Surprisingly, Dmitri knows that she gives him the money hoping that he will spend it in just such a fashion.

The fact is that Katerina will stop at nothing to get even with Dmitri for the insult of that respectful bow. She plans to accomplish this by destroying his honor and shaming him before everyone. And she will stop at nothing to gain her ends. When Dmitri is brought to trial for murdering his father, she willingly destroys her own reputation in order to incriminate him. Furthermore, she produces new evidence that will send Dmitri to Siberia. All this she does, unconsciously, it must be stressed, in order to bring Dmitri to her feet ruined and shamed before all just so she can demonstrate her nobility by forgiving him and thus pay back the insult.

The only thought that distresses Katerina is the prospect of a Dmitri who does not want to be forgiven. This is why she becomes irrational when Alyosha tells her that Dmitri "sends his compliments." Within the context of their relationship, the meaning is unmistakable. The Russian word for this expression means "to say goodby" and also "to bow and be done with bowing." It refers to the bow he made on that certain night. In other words, he breaks the engagement.

All Together

In this chapter Dostoyevsky introduces both Katerina and Grushenka for the first time. Katerina has invited Grushenka to visit so that she can persuade Grushenka to give Dmitri up. But as Alyosha foresees, the meeting between the two women ends unpleasantly because Katerina's image of Grushenka is just as unrealistic as is her image of Dmitri. Katerina imagines her rival as a noble person who plans to forgive her former Polish suitor and marry him, conveniently leaving Dmitri to her. Grushenka, however, reveals herself not to be "an angel" at all. She rejects Katerina and her fantasies, and ends by telling her that she knows all about her visit to Dmitri. Humiliated beyond endurance, Katerina becomes hysterical.

Another Reputation Ruined

Returning to the monastery, Alyosha meets Dmitri, who has been waiting for him, and tells him what has just happened between the two women. Dmitri's laughter indicates that at this point he has decided to degrade himself completely. Unknown to both Alyosha and the reader, Dmitri has fifteen hundred rubles of the original three thousand given him by Katerina in a little bag tied round his neck. As the symbol of his honor, he can either give it back and redeem himself or spend it and so "opt for Sodom." He leaves Alyosha in no doubt about his intentions: "I can still pull up; if I do, I can give back the full half of my lost honor tomorrow. But I shan't pull up. I shall carry out my base plan.... Darkness and destruction! ... The filthy backalley and the she-devil."

THE BROTHERS KARAMAZOV

PART TWO

. . . .

BOOK IV

Pleasure Through Self-Inflicted Suffering

The Russian title for Book IV is Nadryv for which there is no adequate translation in English. One translator renders it as "Heartache" while another uses "Lacerations." Both are misleading. The word derives from the verb nadryvat and can mean "to tear to pieces" or "to injure oneself through over exertion." Dostoyevsky adds a further dimension which might appear like this in a dictionary: "to hurt one's own feelings for the pleasure of it." According to Dostoyevsky there is pleasure in suffering. Many of his heroes seek it out and when they cannot find it, imagine it. The Underground Man, for example, deliberately put himself in the lieutenant's path for no other reason than to have the pleasure of being humiliated. Self-inflicted suffering, or as we may now say, spiritual masochism, is the **theme** of Book IV and is at the root of Ferapont's asceticism, Katerina's love, and Snegiryov's honor.

Father Ferapont is a half crazy, crochety old monk of seventy-five who lives at the monastery in a tiny cubicle behind the beehives. He spends all day kneeling in prayer, rarely speaks, never attends mass, and disapproves of the institution of elders, particularly of Father Zossima. He lives on nothing but bread and water. And very little of that. Consequently, he has hallucinations which he chooses to regard as visions. Most of the monks are afraid of him and all of them feel guilty because they are incapable of his asceticism. We learn, however, that there is a selfish purpose in all of Ferapont's deprivations. His self-denial is not religiously motivated but a special form of masochism. By hurting himself, he hurts the other monks, a sensation that he enjoys. Ferapont needs them in the same way Katerina needs a humiliated Dmitri and Snegiryov needs the two hundred rubles to grind under his boot.

The scene between Katerina, Ivan, and Alyosha presents the phenomenon of masochism from a different angle. Despite the fact that Katerina has suffered a grievous insult from Dmitri through Grushenka, she is firmly resolved to forgive him "and never abandon him." For the rest of her life, she declares hysterically, she will watch over him like a goddess. In Chapter 5 of Book IV she looks forward to the pleasure in store for her as Dmitri's door mat: "I will become nothing but a means for his happiness ... an instrument, a machine for his happiness, and that for my whole life, my whole life, and that he may see that his whole life." Clearly, Katerina has no genuine affection for Dmitri. Her "love" for him is a love of her own suffering. The more he insults her, the more she likes it, and the more she loves him. Nor does she want him to change. She loves him precisely because he insults her. If Dmitri reformed, she would give him up and cease caring about him. She needs him in order to admire her own heroic fidelity in the face of humiliation. When Alyosha tells her this, she flushes crimson, then turns white, her lips quivering in anger. Such is not the reaction of outraged innocence but the sting of truth.

Captain Snegiryov provides the final example of man's capacity for masochism. This man had been forced against his will to take part in Fyodor's underhanded scheme to have Dmitri arrested and locked up for not paying his debts. One day Dmitri sees Snegiryov in a tavern and to have his revenge, he grabs him by the beard and pulls him down the street in this fashion. The Captain's nine-year-old son Ilusha, along with his schoolmates, happens to be passing at the same time and so the father is forced to endure the additional agony of being humiliated before his son. Subsequently, he loses the boy's respect because he does not challenge Dmitri to a duel. When Katerina hears about the incident, she asks Alyosha to take the Captain two hundred rubles as a token of her regret. At first the man is delighted. Having lived most of his life in poverty and burdened moreover by a crippled daughter and a half-witted wife, he could put the money to good use. But at the height of his excitement a sudden change comes over him. He crumples the notes, throws them in the dirt, and begins trampling them shouting all the while: "So much for your money." Then drawing himself up, he tells the bewildered Alyosha that his honor is not for sale. The Captain deliberately hurts himself because of the honorable image he has of himself at that moment.

Alyosha As Christ Figure

The events of Book IV show why Zossima tells Alyosha he must leave the monastery and live within the world. Although

Alyosha never understands why the elder wants him to do this or even what he should do in the world, a brief examination of how he interacts with others will show the wisdom of Zossima's decision.

Alyosha has that rare quality that enables him to bring comfort to the afflicted. Possessed of genuine feeling and true compassion, he is able to soothe the wounds that people inflict upon one another. In fact, he moves among the warring parties something like a Christ figure, grieving inwardly at man's capacity for brutality and self-torment. He stands for truth and fair play, refuses to pass judgment, and appears incapable of anger. For instance, when Katerina calls him "a religious little idiot" for pointing out the true reasons behind her abominable treatment of Ivan, his only reaction is to wring his hands and wonder what to do. And again, when Ilusha hits him with a stone and then viciously bites his finger to the bone, he tries to calm the boy's wrath and find out what has made him act in this way. Ilusha's reaction to Alyosha's refusal to pay back his brutality dramatizes why Zossima sends Alyosha into the world: the boy breaks off the attack and runs away in tears. Alyosha has broken the circle of hurt-and-be-hurt.

Circle Of Hurt-And-Be-Hurt

One of Dostoyevsky's most articulate commentators takes note of the way the author's characters respond to being hurt. Whenever a person is hurt, he immediately seeks to pay it back. In this novel everyone is constantly paying things back. Katerina hurts Dmitri's pride and so he takes revenge by humiliating her. Since she cannot really insult Dmitri, she tortures Ivan. Lise tortures her mother being a brat because she is confined to a wheelchair. Grushenka broods over getting even with her former suitor. Captain Snegiryov hurts Alyosha for his lost honor, while Rakitin writes an insinuating letter to a Petersburg scandal-sheet to pay back an insult from Mme. Hohlakov. And so on. When a person does not act in this way, such as Alyosha, the circle is broken.

In this manner Dostoyevsky dramatizes the effectiveness of Christ's exhortation to "turn the other cheek." He did not consider this a creed for the weak, but rather for the strong. Until people stop trying to pay one another back, the world will continue to devour itself in a manner similar to that presented in this novel. Thus Alyosha resembles Christ most closely when he tries to persuade people to break the circle of hurt-and-be-hurt.

BOOK V

Theme

The central section of Book V, "Rebellion" and "The Grand Inquisitor" is one of the most powerful indictments against God ever written. Dostoyevsky rightly called it "the culminating point of the novel."

Ivan's Scrapbook

In the chapter "Rebellion" Ivan tells Alyosha that he is unable to accept God because He allows such terrible and pointless suffering in the world. To make his case clearer, Ivan has compiled a dossier containing stories and anecdotes gathered from various sources illustrating man's cruelty toward children. His favorite is the one about the little girl of five who, for no apparent reason, was hated by her father and mother, people of education and breeding. With relish either parent beats and kicks the child for the slightest infraction. This cruelty knows no bounds. When one night the child wets the bed, the mother smears excrement over her face, fills her mouth with it, and then locks her up all night in the privy.

Ivan's story about the little serf boy is equally vivid. One day this child of eight throws a stone in play and injures the foot of the master's favorite dog. The general orders him seized and locked up for the night. Next morning he arrives with several hundred of his hounds, his dependent, and family to observe the administration of justice. The boy is stripped naked and told to run. Then the general sets the whole pack of dogs after him and before the mother's eyes the shrieking child is torn to pieces.

Ivan is outraged at the existence of such undeserved suffering. And nothing can justify it, especially not the Christian claim that when mankind reaches the Golden Age everything will be explained and mankind will proclaim "Thou art just O Lord, for Thy ways are revealed." To accept this means to be blind to the present in favor of some future justification. Ivan demands justice now: "And not in some remote infinite time and space, but here on earth.... I want to see it, and if I am dead by then, let me rise again, for if it all happens without me, it will be too unfair. Surely, I haven't suffered simply that I ... may manure the soil of the future harmony for somebody else."

Finally, Ivan says that regardless of how beautiful this future harmony might be, even if he too is resurrected at the Last Judgment and everything is accounted for, he will reject it. Future harmony is not worth the tears of even one suffering child. If this is the price that has to be paid for harmony, he wants no part of it. Instead, he will return "the entrance ticket" to this harmony and turn his back on God.

Sensing that his disquisition is too hypothetical, Ivan brings his ideas into the realm of personal experience in the form of a question. Suppose that he, Alyosha, were given the power to bring about universal harmony. There would be no more war, famine or disease, all the sufferings of mankind would be abolished, and everywhere peace and tranquility would prevail. Only first Alyosha would be required to torture to death one small child and erect his edifice on its suffering. Would he consent to be the architect under these conditions? And would he consent to live in such a place knowing the circumstances? For Alyosha, as for Ivan, the answer is "no."

Ivan believes that rather than waste our energy dreaming of some infinite millennium, we should set about creating a society which would at least abolish mankind's physical suffering. This is within the realm of immediate possibility, but it would require that mankind realign its values according to the precepts of the Grand Inquisitor.

Legend Of The Grand Inquisitor

"The Legend," as it is called for short, constitutes the structural principle of the work. The book is grouped around its ideas like variations on a musical **theme**. Each chapter as well as every incident is a comment or elaboration upon what the Inquisitor says.

"The Legend" is a narrative poem in which the Grand Inquisitor speaks in the first person. The time and place is fifteenth-century Seville during the worst days of the Spanish Inquisition.

Into this setting Ivan introduces Christ. It is not His Second Coming, but a visit as it were. Appearing in His traditional form, He is recognized at once. As He moves along the street, a throng gathers behind Him. Men and women weep, others struggle to touch his garments. The crowd arrives before a Church from which is being carried a small child in a coffin. Voices shout: "He will raise your child," and in fact Christ raises the child. The little girl sits up in her coffin and looks about smiling. There are screams and shouts of hallelujah.

At that particular moment the Grand Inquisitor passes. He watches from a distance for several minutes and when he sees Christ raise the dead child, he orders the Holy Guard to seize Him and lock Him up. Such is the authority of the Inquisitor that the people obediently make way for him and allow Christ to be seized. That night the Inquisitor goes down to the dungeon where Christ is prisoner and talks to Him. He tells Him that he will burn Him the next morning because if anyone ever deserved to be burned as an enemy of the Church, then it should be Christ. Christ, he says, has a great opinion of mankind. As a token of His respect He bestowed upon humanity a great gift, freedom. That is, He gave man a free choice to act or believe in any way he wanted, but with the knowledge of good and evil attached as a condition.

According to the Inquisitor, Christ made a grievous error in so highly esteeming humanity. Nothing has been a greater cause of suffering and disharmony than this gift of freedom because most men are too weak. Several times during the narrative the Inquisitor elaborates upon his opinion of humanity. At one point he observes that "Man is weaker and baser by nature than

Thou hast believed him" while at another he says "he is weak and vile." In short, human beings are ignoble and rebellious while the majority of his actions are motivated by fear and greed. So what did Christ do? Instead of making a gift more in accordance with human nature, He chose "... what was utterly beyond the strength of men.... Instead of taking possession of men's freedom, Thou didst increase it and burdened the spiritual kingdom of mankind with its sufferings for ever." The absurdity of this gift is dramatized by the fact that ninety-nine and forty-four one-hundredths of the world's population cannot even read or write, let alone comprehend something as abstract as freedom. Moreover, history bears out the Inquisitor's view: "Look round and judge; fifteen centuries have passed, look upon them. Whom hast Thou raised up to Thyself?"

What human beings really want out of life is to be fed, to be entertained, and to be told what to do. This concept he formulates in the triadic miracle, mystery, authority. So the Church, understanding the true nature of humanity, has "corrected" Christ's work by changing the basis of Christianity from freedom to food, entertainment, and authority. He maintains that this is the only socio-religious construct that can guarantee universal happiness.

Christ is told that to achieve happiness, man must have his ethics posited for him in terms that he can understand and, most important, easily follow. Yet at the same time, he has to be convinced that he is indeed free to choose. The goal is reached in a diabolically clever manner: to the freedom of moral choice the Inquisitor simply attaches a reward (food) for doing good, and a severe punishment (the Inquisition) for doing the wrong thing. It is a fact of the human condition that most men are more likely to choose between reward and punishment than between good and evil. Finally, when Church and State are accepted as the interpreters of morality, they can simply decree what is right and wrong and so gradually bring humanity round to believe what the rulers think it ought to believe to be happy.

From one point of view the Inquisitor and the Church that he represents can be praised for their realistic approach in creating a kind of heaven on earth. But when we read his description of life in the future society, we see that he wants to turn human beings into little children: "Then we shall give them the quiet humble happiness of weak creatures such as they are by nature.... We shall show them that they are weak, that they are only pitiful children, but that childlike happiness is the sweetest of all. They will become timid and will look to us and huddle close to us in fear, as chicks to the hen. They will marvel at us and will be awestricken before us, and will be proud at our being so powerful and clever, that we have been able to subdue such a turbulent flock of thousands of millions. They will tremble impotently before our wrath, their minds will grow fearful, they will be quick to shed tears like women and children..."

Freedom Or Happiness?

The Grand Inquisitor's plan for the enslavement of mankind is ultimately meant to establish through coercion what freedom has failed to do. Humanity would be free from hunger, disease, and sordid living conditions. Every desire would be satisfied, every destructive instinct domesticated, and every ambition coordinated. Society would function with clock-like precision and everywhere law and order would prevail.

In other words, the Grand Inquisitor claims to be striving for humanity's welfare, concluding that the happiness best suited to human nature is the soothing oblivion of a decisionless existence. Dostoyevsky here illustrates that such a philosophy can lead to the ultimate stage of deterioration, where freedom and the worth of the individual are no longer respected. Church and State carried the concept of apostolic succession, the imitation of Christ and Peter, to a logical and satanic conclusion. After Christ made men free, the ruling authority declared itself the protector of their freedom, thus depriving them of it. In so doing, it destroyed both the effect and reality of freedom and negated the meaning of Christ's life on earth. His coming was therefore useless. In this way the philosophy of the Inquisitor becomes the basis of negation. And religion, by its very nature, becomes inquisitorial. By withdrawing freedom, the Church, or any central authority, gradually deprives mankind of its individuality and creativity and thus becomes an instrument of disintegration and decay.

Preparations For Murder

The last two chapters of Book V reveal the extent of Ivan's involvement with Smerdyakov and show the manner in which Ivan gives his consent to his father's murder. First we learn that just after arriving in town Ivan spent considerable time with Smerdyakov discussing philosophy and religion. At first he likes Smerdyakov, encourages him to speak, and finds him original. They discuss Ivan's ethical theories and the supposition that "if there is no God, then everything is lawful," an idea that Smerdyakov finds particularly attractive. During the last few days, however, Ivan begins to feel an intense dislike, almost hatred for his half-brother because of certain recent changes in his behavior. Smerdyakov has assumed an air of revolting familiarity toward Ivan, as if there existed an understanding between them, a secret, or unspoken agreement known only to them alone, and beyond the comprehension of those around them. Delving further into the reasons for his sudden dislike, Ivan remembers that of late Smerdyakov has shown signs of a boundless and wounded vanity and that this lies behind certain, enigmatic questions which he asks, the true meanings of which Ivan cannot uncover. All of these thoughts occur to Ivan the moment he sees Smerdyakov sitting on a bench in front of the house. Although his first impulse is to call him a miserable idiot, he is seized by a will seemingly not his own which forces him to address his brother in a friendly manner and to sit down on the bench to talk. A remarkable conversation now takes place.

What the brothers say to each other must be read on two levels. On the surface, Smerdyakov's remarks appear to be nothing more than stilted pleasantries touching on many different subjects. He speaks about Chermashnaya and Fyodor's insistence that Ivan go there on an errand for him, then he mentions the old man's passion for Grushenka, comments on Dmitri's hatred for Fyodor, speculates whether an epileptic can predict a seizure, and finishes his chatter by revealing his desire to open a restaurant in Moscow. A closer look at these remarks reveals that Smerdyakov is telling Ivan that final preparations for the murder have been made and that Ivan should go to Chermashnaya to establish his alibi. To put himself in the clear, he will simulate an epileptic fit. Then that night he will gain entry to the house by using the secret signals that are intended to announce Grushenka's arrival, murder the old man, arrange things so that the blame falls on Dmitri, and finally take the three thousand rubles meant for Grushenka to open a restaurant in Moscow.

Ivan's reaction to Smerdyakov's proposal is a study in psychology. While the social side of Ivan's nature revolts against the idea, another, more elemental, part of himself is so exhilarated at the prospect of his father's death that it blocks his perception.

Of course, the real Ivan knows the truth, but he pretends not to understand Smerdyakov's insinuations, pretends that he does not wish his father's death, and pretends that his sudden decision to leave town has nothing to do with the affair. But he flatly refuses to go to Chermashnaya. To do so would mean admitting to himself that he knows all about the crime and approves of it. Yet he cannot remain in town either, for that would indicate disapproval. So he goes to Moscow. This, of course, is no more than an exercise in self-deception because it is his departure, not his destination, that gives Smerdyakov the signal to kill Fyodor. Were further examples needed to prove Ivan's complicity, we need only quote his answer to Fyodor's urgent request that he go to Chermashnaya: "So, you force me to go there yourself."

In other terms, Ivan wants Smerdyakov to kill his father but he does not want to be involved himself because he lacks the courage of his convictions. What does this tell us about the man who proclaims that "all things are lawful" and who looks down upon the masses for their inability to make a free choice and accept the responsibility? It shows that he is lying to himself.

Although self-deception protects Ivan for a while, his conscience gnaws away at him until finally in Book XII he will perceive the invalidity of his ideas, his responsibility in Fyodor's death, and the magnitude of his dishonesty. Overwhelmed, he sinks into madness.

BOOK VI

Theme

The Brothers Karamazov was first published serially in the conservative journal *The Russian Messenger*. When the chapter

"The Grand Inquisitor" appeared, the patriarch of the Russian Church was so upset by the force of the Inquisitor's arguments that he wrote the author to inquire how these arguments would be met. Dostoyevsky answered that the refutation would appear in the next issue of the journal and that it would be entitled "The Russian Monk." Dostoyevsky was worried about its success because he knew that this section lacks the power of the Inquisitor chapter. In general, though, he was not concerned since on another occasion he remarked that "the whole book serves as an answer."

Doctrine Of Love And Suffering

Opposite the Inquisitor's Euclidian estimate of human nature and Ivan's proclamation that all things are lawful stands Zossima's evocation of human worth and his assertion that "all are responsible for all." His solution for solving the problem of man and his relationship to society is based on the principle of love and suffering. He, as Dostoyevsky, believes in a "universal guilt" by which he means that each individual bears the guilt of all men, and when he suffers, for any reason, expiates some of that guilt. Enduring anguish for the sins of mankind becomes an obligation of Dostoyevsky's characters. And if they achieve redemption at the end, it is through both suffering and love. The love that is important to Zossima is not selfish love, but caritas, a feeling which can best be described as a love for all men, for all life, and for all things. There can be no limit to caritas. Zossima's theodicy is connected with the measure of man's love, and he believes that all the guilt and suffering in the world can be absorbed in universal love. He says that if mankind is to gain happiness on earth, each individual must base his actions on caritas: "Love God's creation, the whole, and every grain of sand in it…. If you love everything, you will perceive the divine mystery in things." Zossima relates three stories from his life to illustrate what he means.

The first story is about his elder brother Markel. When Markel was seventeen he became a freethinker, blasphemed against God, and looked upon religion as an opiate of the masses. Much like Ivan, he rejected all ethical standards not his own, saw human society as wasteful, futile, and disordered. He was rarely satisfied and usually in bad spirits. Then he became mortally ill with consumption. As the disease racked his body, he discovered a peace and joy in life that he had never known. Through suffering, he arrived at an understanding of it and gained insight into its value. He died at peace with himself and the world.

Zossima's account of his own early life looks at the problem from another angle. As a young artillery officer, he delighted in drink and riot. Inevitably, he fell in love and spent considerable time paying court to the girl. But such was the extent of his youthful conceit and reluctance to abandon the life of a carefree bachelor, he procrastinated in making her an offer. Then his unit was sent for two months to another district. Upon his return, he discovered that not only had the girl married, but she had been betrothed during the time he was courting her. Fancying he had made a fool of himself and that everyone was laughing behind his back, Zossima found a pretext and challenged the husband to a duel. But the morning of the event he underwent a remarkable transformation watching the sun rise.

Suddenly viewing himself in perspective, he saw to what depths he had sunk, and decided to change his ways. At the duel, he calmly received his opponent's shot, flung his own unfired weapon into the forest, and then begged his adversary's forgiveness. That same day he resigned his commission with the intention of entering a monastery. Not from sorrow or fear but from joy. During the month before his discharge, he was enthusiastically received into all the best houses where he explained the reasons for his transformation and elaborated upon his favorite saying that everyone is responsible for all: "You may well not know it since the whole world has long been going on a different line, since we consider the veriest lies as truths and demand the same lies from others. Here I have for once in my life acted sincerely and, well, you all look upon me as a madman. Though you are friendly to me, yet, you see, you all laugh at me." But there was one person who did not laugh.

Mikhail's Story

Mikhail, a mysterious man usually present at these gatherings, listened intensely to everything that Zossima said. Soon he took to visiting him at home and several weeks revealed the reasons for his interest. Fourteen years previously this man had murdered the woman he loved because she wanted to marry another. The blame fell upon a servant who died in prison of a fever before he could be brought to trial. For fourteen years Mikhail suffered the agony of conscience. He married and had children hoping to escape from the memories. But each year he grew more troubled until that deed poisoned his life altogether. This accounted for his interest in Zossima. He wanted to discover how Zossima found the strength of character to serve the truth even at the risk of incurring everyone's contempt. He, too, wanted to tell the truth and suffer the punishment prescribed by society so that he could expiate his sin. Finally, with Zossima's example as his guide, he made a full confession both to society and to the legal authorities. The town, however, preferred to believe that he had fallen mentally ill and that his confession was no more than the ravings of a madman. In fact, he did fall ill a few days after the confession and died. On his deathbed he told Zossima: "There was heaven in my heart from the moment I had done what I had to do. Now I dare to love my children and to kiss them."

Salvation Through Suffering

Dostoyevsky's primary objective is to show that the repentant sinner is able to gain redemption only through voluntarily accepting suffering. Moreover, in Mikhail's condemnation of himself we see how the moral law is fulfilled because, in his new attitude, he attains to respect and humility before the moral law and thereby gives essence to the law. Since Mikhail was miserable in the awareness of his guilt, and since he wanted to suffer voluntarily the punishment in order to forgive himself, he made his confession.

Nature Of Suffering

Dostoyevsky firmly believed in the regenerative power of suffering, considering it essential for the expiation of guilt. Furthermore, suffering voluntarily accepted leads to spiritual rebirth. The nature of suffering and its role in Dostoyesvky's novels will be clearer if we pause to consider its position in Russian thought.

Ranking as one of the chief characteristics of Russian Orthodoxy is mysticism, the belief in the possibility of direct communion with God. This communion does not depend on any outside factors such as revelation, or answers to prayers. Rather the highest communion is achieved by direct imitation, or identification which enables the soul to partake of the divine essence. The mystic accepts symbolism as literally or metaphysically true. In this state of mind, God ceases to be an idea and becomes an experience. Since Christ's greatest moment on earth was His suffering and death for humanity, the Russian feels that when he suffers he approaches Christ in both a mystical and literal sense.

This mystical-religious disposition and the belief in the absolutism of suffering is a result of the peculiar history of Russia. It is one of suffering. Christianity was the people's only comfort during the centuries of immeasurable hardship when it was at the mercy of other nations. The traditions and legends of the people emphasize the conviction that the weak, the insulted and the injured will, at the Last Judgment, be exalted above the domineering aristocracy from whom they endured such anguish. The dictum "The meek shall inherit the earth" has real meaning for them.

The Russian ideal then finds expression in suffering as a spiritual bond between men and God. If we consider for a moment the actions and life of Christ, we can better understand the significance of this bond. The difference between the Old and the New Testament determines man's relationship both to himself and to humanity at large. The Ten Commandments are concerned chiefly with actions, whereas Jesus' law focuses on feeling - the love of God and one's neighbor. If action is subordinated to feeling, the concepts of sin, freedom, and the law undergo a basic change. As Christianity developed in the West, however, the importance of actions rather than states of mind continued to be stressed. According to Jesus, laws can be fulfilled only through humility and love. He had infinite patience with thieves, drunkards, and harlots and reserved his wrath for the Scribes and Pharisees whose actions might have been irreproachable but whose feelings and minds were corrupt. Likewise, Dostoyevsky portrayed murderers, prostitutes, and alcoholics as basically good people whereas he viciously attacks men of empty actions, merchants, bureaucrats, and the whole hypocritical middle class. The Russian interpretation of Christianity, therefore, emphasizes the inner man, his feelings and his state of mind.

A final aspect of suffering yet to be considered concerns its regenerative value. From his study of the Bible, Dostoyevsky learned that God communicates with man in two ways: through visions and through the infliction of suffering. This suffering may be physical in nature as in Job's case or it may be purely spiritual such as that experienced by King David. In every case the aim of this suffering is to cause the good man to see the error of his ways and return to God who then forgives him. In his novels Dostoyevsky modernized this concept by equating spiritual anguish with the pain of bad conscience and by substituting the sinner's own self-forgiveness for God's redemption. Rodion Raskolnikov illustrates this point. Immediately after he kills the old moneylender he is overwhelmed by such pangs of conscience that it soon threatens to destroy his mental equilibrium. To expiate the transgression, Raskolnikov confesses to the police and accepts the punishment. At the end of the novel he forgives himself and in so doing undergoes a spiritual rebirth. Thus suffering is more than temporal salvation. It is the death, resurrection, and rebirth of the real and free human being.

THE BROTHERS KARAMAZOV

. . . .

BOOK VII

No Miracle

In Book V, the Grand Inquisitor rebukes Christ: "Thos didst hope that man, following Thee, would cling to God and not ask for a miracle. But Thou didst know that when man rejects miracle he rejects God too; for man seeks not so much God as the miraculous." The manner in which the townspeople and the monks conduct themselves at Zossima's funeral bears out the unfortunate truth of this statement.

Since Zossima was widely regarded as a saint while he was alive, many people expect a sign or miracle to accompany his death. A rumor to this effect sweeps the town and by noon crowds of people assemble near the monastery expecting to witness something spectacular. Some bring their sick, confident that the dead elder's remains have the power of healing. The monks in particular are gripped by excitement. Instead of a miracle, though, Zossima begins to stink. Even his most devoted followers are dismayed by this turn of events partly because it is widely believed that holy men do not putrefy. This event brings down a shower of abuse from Zossima's enemies.

The elder's critics point out that he has begun to decay in less than twelve hours while even an ordinary sinner does not begin the process until at least twenty-four. They swiftly conclude that this premature corruption must be the long-awaited sign from Heaven and should be interpreted as an expression of God's disapproval. Cheated of a miracle, the monks invent one of their own. The Grand Inquisitor continues: "And as man cannot bear to be without the miraculous, he will create new miracles of his own."

When Father Ferapont hears about the premature decay, he seizes the opportunity to pay Zossima back for being more popular than he. With chains clanking and cassock fluttering, he storms into the elder's cell casting out devils left and right and calling upon all to behold the finger of God. Working himself into a spiritual frenzy, he screams, shouts, gesticulates, and finally falls face down into the dirt where he babbles incoherently. Not surprisingly, some of the monks look upon this spectacle as the sign from Heaven.

In this **episode** Dostoyevsky shows that Ferapont, the townspeople as well as the monks neither comprehend what it means to be a Christian nor what it is that made Zossima saintly. A Christian to Dostoyevsky is a man that loves life, is at peace with himself, and cares about his fellow man. Zossima's saintliness is a manifestation of his love and compassion. Alyosha will be the only one present at the funeral who is permitted to understand. But before he has this experience, he must undergo a severe trial.

Alyosha's Revulsion

The events of the funeral affect Alyosha profoundly. Like the others, he experiences a sense of revulsion when Zossima begins to decay in front of everybody. Having stood in a position of such reverence to Zossima, he too secretly expected something to happen at his death. If not a miracle, then something befitting the occasion. But there is no miracle, and the man who should have been exalted by the people is suddenly degraded and dishonored by them. It is this that mortifies Alyosha. He cannot understand why God allows this holy man to be jeered and humiliated by a crowd so inferior to him. Why this indignity? Why is everyone so eager to slander Zossima's life? Unable to comprehend the ways of Providence and grieved over his teacher's ignominious treatment, Alyosha begins to murmur against God. Echoing Ivan he tells Rakitin: "I am not rebelling against my God. I simply don't accept his world." Now long-suppressed drives held in check by his awe of Zossima suddenly rise to the surface and for a time threaten to engulf him.

Rakitin, A Miniature Mephistopheles

Like Alyosha, Rakitin is a novice at the monastery. Unlike him, Rakitin has chosen the Church as a career not from any profound religious convictions but because this offers him the best chance for advancement. And he never undertakes anything without the prospect of gain. He caters to people in power and he will accommodate himself to any project or circumstance if he detects the slightest advantage from doing so. He naturally assumes that everyone else is acting the same way. For example, when Zossima bows to Dmitri in Book II, Rakitin interprets the action as a farsighted scheme to enhance his reputation as a prophet. For should Dmitri kill Fyodor, which appears to be likely, people will remember the bow and nod sagely that Zossima saw it all in advance. Although Rakitin's base view of humanity is borne out only too well by the townspeople and the monks, Alyosha is different. Rakitin dislikes anyone whose motives are genuine. Thus when he sees that Alyosha is susceptible to temptation, he at once recognizes how he can profit from it. He remembers that on several occasions Grushenka asked him to bring Alyosha to her because she would like to seduce him and see his innocent face corrupted with sensual lust. In doing this, not only would Rakitin have the satisfaction of seeing Alyosha fall from grace, he would also collect the twenty-five ruble bribe from Grushenka.

At Grushenka's

In this scene Dostoyevsky shows how Grushenka's life is dominated by hatred and a desire for revenge. Soon after their arrival Grushenka, instead of carrying out her plan of seduction, is overcome by a paroxysm of self-loathing and confesses to Alyosha her inmost secrets. She tells him that at seventeen she was seduced by a Polish officer who abandoned her. The officer moved to another district and married, leaving her in poverty and disgrace. Subsequently, she was "bought" by Kuzma Samsonov, a businessman renowned for his parsimony. During the first years of her bondage she would shut herself in every evening and indulge in a veritable orgy of self-pity, sobbing at the injustice of her fate, her disgrace, and the hopelessness of her position. Now after five years this man writes to say that he is widowed and is coming to see her. But Grushenka is not in a forgiving mood. She enjoys hating him, she cultivates it and broods over how she will "pay him out."

Grushenka's thirst for revenge has brought all her baser qualities to the surface. On the one hand she has become hard-hearted, cunning, and often delights in taking unfair advantage when engaging in business affairs. At the same time she is morbidly sensitive about her sinful ways. It is because of this that she develops an irrational dislike of Alyosha, imagining that he is silently passing judgment on her. She particularly dislikes the way he always drops his eyes when they meet on the street, or how he purposely avoids meeting her. She aches to pay him back by corrupting him and robbing him of his dignity. And finally, she confesses how lowly she regards herself for having these thoughts: "Do you see now, Alyosha, what a vile, vindictive creature I am?" But Alyosha neither regards her as base nor does he judge. Instead, he appeals to her higher nature which no one, including herself, thought she possessed. He tells her that she will not succumb to her evil longing for revenge because of her basically good nature and that she will join her Polish officer in a forgiving mood.

The Whole Novel Is An Answer

Here is the first indication of Dostoyevsky's indirect refutation of the Grand Inquisitor's view of man. Alyosha's love and compassion overcomes Grushenka's hatred and desire for revenge. Her self-respect restored, she forgets her vindictiveness and forgives the man who caused her such grief.

Miracle That Does Happen

A miracle does occur after all but it is presented in terms of a dream. Alyosha returns to the monastery and immediately goes to where Father Paissy is reading over Zossima's body. He is reading the story of Christ's first miracle, the turning of water into wine. He falls asleep and in his dream the funeral rites merge into the wedding feast at which Alyosha now finds himself. The elder, too, is present and alive at the celebration. He takes Alyosha and explains the meaning of Christ's miracle. Christ always worked His miracles to increase man's gladness and his religion is one of joy, not of sadness. He explains: "He has made Himself like unto us from love and rejoices with us. He is changing the water into wine that the gladness of the guests may not be cut short." So finally Alyosha understands why Zossima told him "to sojourn in the world." He, like Christ, knows how to increase a person's gladness.

BOOK VIII

Theme

Dmitri now looks upon his love for Grushenka as something more than a passionate obsession. It is an opportunity to break out of his dissolute existence and begin life anew. Dmitri's first truly moral act is the decision to repay the three thousand he owes Katerina, for this debt functions as the symbol of his former existence. (The Russian word for debt and guilt is the same.) Or in other terms, paying his debts will signify his break with the past. This is not an easy task since he has only fifteen hundred.

Dmitri's Frustration

In the first five chapters, Dmitri dashes about in futile, frenetic attempts to get the money. First he goes to Samsonov with a harebrained scheme to sell the merchant his non-existent rights to the village Chermashnaya. The manner in which he addresses Samsonov indicates the true state of his mind. His speech is incoherent, he glosses over his legal rights to the village, and ends by begging the old man to give him the three thousand today, this morning, immediately if not sooner, whichever comes first. But Samsonov grasps the situation in an instant. He sees that Dmitri is a man on the brink of ruin, vainly grasping at straws in an effort to save himself. In the second place, the merchant loves Grushenka himself and does not want to see her carried off by this "swaggering idler." So he revenges himself by sending Dmitri off on a wild-goose chase. He tells him to contact the peasant Lygavy, now in the district, and make the same proposal to him. Broke, Dmitri sells his watch, pawns his dueling pistols, hires a cart, and drives twenty miles into the countryside to see the peasant who, as it happens, has just decided to get drunk and stay that way for the next week. Dmitri rushes back to town empty-handed and tries to borrow the money from the scatterbrained Mme. Hohlakov who tediously urges him to go work the Siberian goldmines.

As Dmitri is leaving Mme. Hohlakov's house, he meets one of Samsonov's servants and discovers that Grushenka is not sitting with the old man as she promised and that she left ten minutes after she had arrived at his place. The ensuing events figure among the novel's most crucial for they establish the circumstantial evidence that will convict Dmitri of Fyodor's murder and at the same time mark the death of the old Dmitri, the destruction of the Karamazov spirit within him, and indicate the first stages of Dmitri's rebirth.

Fyodor's Death

As soon as Dmitri hears that Grushenka lied to him concerning her whereabouts, he immediately assumes that she has gone to spend the night with Fyodor. He dashes there, scales the garden wall, and sneaks up to the lighted window. To find out for sure if Grushenka is there, he taps the secret code on the windowpane learned from Smerdyakov that announces "Grushenka has come." The old man leans out the window calling her name eagerly. Here occurs the second indirect refutation of the Grand Inquisitor's judgment of mankind. Although overcome by jealousy, revulsion, and hatred for his father, he finds within himself the power to resist the murderous impulse. His troubles, though, are far from over. Meanwhile, Grigory, awakened by the noise, comes out into the garden in time to grab Dmitri's leg just as he is scrambling back over the wall. Dmitri knocks the old servant unconscious with the brass pestle he had snatched up at Grushenka's a few minutes earlier. He jumps down to see after Grigory, tries to mop up the blood with his handkerchief, and ends by getting it all over himself. But Dmitri has no time to worry about the blood because he is driven by his passion to find Grushenka. Vaulting over the wall, he runs back to her house where he finds out from the servants that she has gone to Mokroe to see her former suitor. While all this is going on Smerdyakov gets up, murders Fyodor, and makes it back to his bed unseen. This fact, however, is revealed three hundred pages later in Book XI.

The discovery of Grushenka's whereabouts brings about a complete change in Dmitri. His insane jealousy and the ensuing frantic activity give way to resignation when he at last understands the finality of her decision. His dream of a new life shattered, he decides to shoot himself. But first he wants to see Grushenka once more. Dmitri reaches the lowest moral point when he takes Katerina's fifteen-hundred rubles from the pouch round his neck to finance one last celebration with Grushenka and her lover. Since he needs his pistols to execute his plan, he first goes to Perhotin to redeem them. His peculiar behavior, bloodspattered clothes, and most of all his sudden riches arouse

Perhotin's suspicions, and a few hours after Dmitri's visit, he goes to the police.

On The Road To Mokroe

On the way to Mokroe, Dmitri makes a remarkable prayer to God. This prayer reveals that while his outward actions appear base, brutal, and dishonest, the inner man has not lost sight of the ideal and is struggling to assert himself. "Lord, receive me, with all my lawlessness and do not condemn me. Let me pass by Thy judgment ... do not condemn me, for I have condemned myself, do not condemn me, for I love Thee, O Lord. I am a wretch, but I love Thee. If Thou sendest me to hell, I shall love Thee there, and from there I shall cry out that I love Thee for ever and ever." Here again Dostoyevsky repeats the **theme** of man's broadness, the amazing capacity of human nature to combine within itself two polar opposites, the ideal of Sodom and the ideal of the Madonna. Yet before Dmitri can defeat the spirit of the Karamazov's once and for all and enter upon a life of joy and happiness, he must first be purified by suffering. It is nevertheless ironic that he is allowed to experience paradise for a few hours before the police arrest him.

First And Rightful Lover

When Dmitri arrives with his wagonload of provisions, he expects to find Grushenka and her lover celebrating their reunion. Instead, they are bored to tears. Her suitor is anything but the suave, Polish aristocrat that we have come to expect. Twice married and five years older, he has gotten fat, grown bald, and looks ridiculous peering out from under his cheap wig: Small wonder that this man soon reveals himself as a self-important, arrogant little nobody who cheats at cards and hates everything Russian, a characteristic that Dostoyevsky reserves only for his most repulsive figures.

Soon after Dmitri's arrival, Grushenka recognizes the Pole for what he is, sees what a fool she has been, and confesses to Dmitri that she loves only him. This turn of events throws the young man into an intoxicating delirium. In typical Russian fashion he sends for musicians and dancing girls, and it's free champagne for everybody. When the celebration reaches its peak and both Dmitri and Grushenka are at the summit of happiness, the police arrive to arrest Dmitri for parricide. Nevertheless, despite this low point in Dmitri's life, his rebirth now begins.

BOOK IX

Theme

The seventy-five pages of Book IX recount Dmitri's interrogation by the authorities. During the course of the investigation first the reader and then Dmitri gradually realize that while there are no incontrovertible facts that prove his guilt, the circumstantial evidence is overwhelming. For instance, everyone in town knows of the son's hatred for his father, has heard him threaten his life, and is familiar with their competition for Grushenka. The most incriminating evidence concerns Dmitri's blood-soaked clothes, the brass pestle, and his money. Since Fyodor was found in a pool of blood with his head bashed in by a blunt instrument, and the pestle was found near the scene of the crime, and since they know that Dmitri picked it up in Grushenka's house, the investigators feel more than justified in their conclusions. Nor can Dmitri convince them of the source of his sudden wealth. Nobody believes the story that he had carried it around his neck for three months. So the authorities accuse him of stealing the money Fyodor had ready for Grushenka's visit, indict him for murder, and lock him up to await trial.

Dmitri's Moral Maturation

The events of Dmitri's official interrogation are secondary to that of his moral maturation which now begins. Up until this time the author emphasizes the childlike dimensions of Dmitri's nature. He is portrayed as frank, sincere, but naive and as such seems beyond good and evil. But Dmitri cannot remain indefinitely in a state of immaturity. The emergence into adulthood is brought about by two experiences, one involving the real world, the other a dream. First, during the interrogation, Dmitri suffers an indignity that deeply affects his ego. He has to strip naked while the authorities examine his clothes. He feels ashamed both for his nakedness and his clothes which, like his present life, are unclean. This experience may also be read in another way. Stripped of his past sins Dmitri, although naked and alone like a newborn babe, is ready to begin life anew. The direction that his new life will take is revealed to him in a dream. It is going to be a life of compassion, of self-sacrifice.

Dmitri dreams that he is a lieutenant in the army once more and that he is being driven across the steppes in winter. The cart passes a burned-out village and beside the road stands a mother holding a new-born babe, its hands and arms purple from the cold. Dmitri weeps and asks the driver why the babe cries, why they don't feed it: "And he felt that a passion of pity, such as he had never known before, was rising in his heart, that he wanted to cry, that he wanted to do something for them all ... that no one should shed tears again from that moment." This dream reveals Dmitri to himself and becomes the turning point in his life. He awakes a different man. Morally reborn, he actually looks forward to the punishment in store for him because he regards the punishment for a crime of which he is innocent as an opportunity to expiate his real sins and those of the world as well. He will suffer for the babe, its mother, in fact for all mankind. He tells the authorities: "Never, never should I have arisen of myself. But the thunderbolt has fallen. I accept the torture of accusation, and my public shame, I want to suffer, and by suffering I shall be purified."

At this point, Dostoyevsky breaks off his narrative of Dmitri's fate to take up a different theme.

BOOK X

Theme

Book X, "The Boys," is a subplot only vaguely connected to the novel. First, it relates the events of Ilusha's illness and then it shows Alyosha's beneficial influence on the schoolboys. Of this group of adolescents it is the precocious Kolya Krassotkin who captures the reader's interest. Although only fourteen, he has the mind of an adult and takes great pride in showing off his intellectual agility. Always first or second in his class, he reads voraciously, and in some instances his knowledge is reputed to exceed that of his teachers. But before he meets Alyosha, he uses his intellect primarily to dominate his schoolmates or to make fools of the peasants. One prank in particular, while apparently harmless, is a variation on the novel's **theme** of guilt. He tells how he induced a simple-minded country bumpkin to drive a cart over a goose's neck. When the two were caught and brought before the Justice of the Peace, the country lad tried to extricate himself by claiming that Kolya egged him on. Kolya tells the magistrate the peasant should be punished because "I simply stated the general proposition, and spoke hypothetically." This incident is a minor illustration of Ivan's guilt in that Kolya, like him, provides the intellectual inspiration for crime. Kolya is by no means an evil person. He has many qualities and the boys follow his example. Sometimes, however, he unintentionally abuses his influence with unfortunate consequences, as in the case of Ilusha Snegiryov.

Ilusha becomes slavishly devoted to Kolya after Kolya rescues him from an unequal fight in the schoolyard. Then one day, when Kolya hears about the way his new friend threw a stray dog a piece of bread with a pin in it for the pleasure of watching him squeal. (It is significant that Ilusha learned this trick from Smerdyakov.) Kolya tells him that he will no longer have anything to do with a person of such low character. By punishing Ilusha he hopes to develop in him the consciousness of his own guilt. This, we recall, is the only form of punishment which Zossima acknowledges. Yet Kolya unknowingly causes Ilusha too much suffering over the dog Zhucka. When Kolya withdraws his favor, the other boys turn on Ilusha and soon injure him in the rock fight which we remember from Book IV. Immediately thereafter he falls ill with consumption. Kolya is aware of his friend's illness, he knows that he is sorry about the dog, and is grieving over the loss of his best friend. Kolya still refuses to visit him. There is a reason for his procrastination.

For the past several weeks Kolya has heard the boys talk about Alyosha who has become a frequent visitor at Ilusha's bedside. With growing irritation Kolya listens to his schoolmates proclaim Alyosha's virtues. Annoyed at this threat to his leadership, he plans to regain his rightful place in a spectacular way. First, he finds the dog that Ilusha had harmed, keeps him locked up at home, and teaches him a variety of tricks. Then he carefully picks a day when he knows that all the boys and Alyosha will be at Ilusha's bedside. Arriving late on purpose, Kolya makes his grand entrance, forgives the boy for his transgressions, and makes him a present of the dog, re-named Perezvon. Naturally, everyone is overawed by Kolya's carefully staged dramatics and there are shouts and cries of joy. Only Alyosha is not impressed for he fears the shock may be too severe for Ilusha's weakened constitution.

So important is Alyosha's approval that Kolya begins to make a vulgar display of his intellect. He tries to impress Alyosha by assuming a blase, sophisticated manner in criticizing the school's curriculum. The study of Latin and Greek is useless, serving only to stupefy the intellect while universal history is dismissed as an arid account of the successive follies of mankind. He ends by questioning the existence of God and viewing Christ as merely "a good man." But Alyosha wins him over by the simple tactic of being himself and accepting Kolya as an equal. In their brief conversation in the hallway, Alyosha's genuineness so disarms the boy that he confesses to showing off, admits how scared he is, and tells Alyosha how much store he set by his friendship. Subsequently, he becomes as devoted to Alyosha as his schoolmates are to him.

In this **episode** Dostoyevsky shows once again why Zossima sends Alyosha to live in the world. Through love and understanding he demolishes the defenses the children have erected about themselves. And through his personal charm he acts as a mediator between the adult world and that of the children just as he previously served as a link between the outside world and the monastery. Thus under Alyosha's influence, Kolya becomes the chief force in transforming the hatred between Ilusha and the other boys into love and a sense of brotherhood.

BOOK XI

Grushenka's Metamorphosis

Grushenka's five-week illness following Dmitri's arrest at Mokroe changes her both physically and spiritually. Thinner and somewhat sallow, her face has taken on a look of firmness and intelligence which reflects this new attitude. Now her frivolity and gay disposition are replaced by a "steadfast and humble determination." What strikes the reader above all are not so much the changes in Grushenka's attitude but Dostoyevsky's strikingly modern portrait of her as a woman.

For the last one hundred years, critics have usually proclaimed Dostoyevsky's portrayal of women as inadequate, insisting that he did not really understand them nor did he know the meaning of true femininity. But if these women are examined in the light of ideas prevailing in the last third of this century, it turns out that Dostoyevsky knew what he was talking about after all. In fact, he may be one of the few male authors of the nineteenth century who did understand them.

Dostoyevsky has little use for the stereotyped woman who plays the role of the soft, fluffy toy whose life revolves about trapping a husband and subsequent immersion into domestic tranquility. When he does portray such types, he uses them as comic relief, as for example Mme. Hohlakov. It is perhaps noteworthy that in his major novels none of the main female characters are married. He portrays them strong, self-reliant, and determined to arrange their lives to suit themselves. Furthermore, there is no necessarily sharp distinction between male and female psychology. His female **protagonists** are just as tortured, cruel, and sadistic or as loving, gentle, and idealistic as his men. Accordingly, though Grushenka loves Dmitri more than anything, she will not permit herself to be dominated by him. When, for instance, after listening to rumors that the two Poles are still in town and that Grushenka has given them small amounts of money, Dmitri accuses her of supporting her former lover on the sly, pretending it is for charity. Grushenka responds by immediately sending the two men some money and food, which she had not planned to do, as a way of asserting her independence. This woman's character stands out in sharp relief to that of Mme. Hohlakov, the next person on Alyosha's itinerary.

Mme. Hohlakov

The real object of Alyosha's visit to the Hohlakov's house concerns Lise, but just as he tries to sneak upstairs, her mother pounces upon him and begins chattering. Alyosha notices that during the last two months she has begun to dress more carefully, that is, more in accordance with what the men of that period were likely to notice. Even though she has a sore foot and cannot get about too well, she receives visitors in an enchanting dress with flounces, ruffles, and frills. What follows is the novel's most comical episode.

Mme. Hohlakov is particularly upset today by an article in Gossip, a Petersburg scandal-sheet specializing in the indiscretions of high society. Since Dmitri's trial has become the talk of all Russia and since the newspapers are interested in the smallest, and preferably juiciest, detail, they have taken note of Dmitri's visit to her to borrow the three thousand rubles. The report, however, is not an accurate representation of the facts: "The criminal was continually involved in amorous intrigues, and particularly popular with certain ladies 'who were pining in solitude.' One such lady, a pining widow, who tried to seem young though she had a grown up daughter, was so fascinated by him that only two hours before the crime she offered him three thousand rubles, on condition that he would elope with her to the gold mines. But the criminal, counting on escaping punishment, had preferred to murder his father to get the three thousand, rather than go off to Siberia with the middle-aged charms of his pining lady." Although no names are mentioned, it is apparent to anyone familiar with the case that "the pining lady" is Mme. Hohlakov. The good humor of this chapter is followed in the next by a chilling scene between Alyosha and Lise.

Little Demon

Lise is the teenage daughter of Mme. Hohlakov whom Alyosha has known since they were in Moscow together. At that time they used to talk about their experiences, ideas, and plans for the future. Finally, they became secretly engaged. In those days Lise had been lovable. But when she contracted a disease that confined her to a wheelchair, she became bitter and resentful toward the world. Cheated of a normal life, she tries to make everyone else's life as miserable as her own. She treats her mother with great disrespect, feigns hysterics to gain attention, and on one occasion strikes a servant. Though she loves Alyosha, she torments him as well. At one moment she accuses him of not loving her; at another of duplicity or even of sanctimoniousness. She knows quite well that if they get married it would only hinder his mission in the world, but this thought only increases her vindictiveness. For the sole purpose of torturing Alyosha, she reveals all her loathsome dreams. And if this were not enough, she hints at an illicit relationship between herself and Ivan. Finally, at the end of the chapter she turns her hatred upon herself. After Alyosha leaves the room, she opens the door, inserts her finger in the crack, and slams it shut. Ten seconds later she takes the finger out and while watching the blood well up from under the crushed nail, she gasps through the pain: "I am a wretch, wretch, wretch."

Only Alyosha's immense capacity for understanding can overcome such self-hatred. He does not waver in his devotion to her. Yet she represents for him another kind of danger, the pull toward the sensualism of the Karamazovs. Here Alyosha is only confronted with the temptation of the flesh. The portrayal of Alyosha's experience with sin is a **theme** Dostoyevsky promised for an unwritten sequel. The great sinner of this novel is Dmitri whom Alyosha now visits in prison.

"A Hymn And A Secret"

This counts as one of the book's most important chapters. When Alyosha arrives at the prison, Dmitri is listening to Rakitin's account of the ideas of the French scientist Claude Bernard. This scientist maintains that all human thinking and feeling is merely the result of chemicals secreted by the body acting upon nerve cells. Thus, such sensations as love, hatred, and sorrow are no more than bio-chemical phenomena. In other words, Claude Bernard reduces not only emotion and thought but also God and the belief in immortality to an equation. While these ideas fascinate Dmitri, he hates them intensely. How, he asks, can his thirst for punishment, his insight into the truth of the dictum that "all are responsible to all," be defined in terms of mathematics? Speculation upon these ideas leads Dmitri back to his favorite subject: suffering.

As we have seen from earlier chapters, he looks forward to the suffering in store for him because he regards it as a sign that

God is giving him a chance to expiate his real sins. But today Ivan, who has been visiting him secretly, places a great burden upon him by proposing that if the jury returns a guilty verdict, he should agree to escape. Rakitin, too, urges him to go along with the plan. Expressed in other terms, Dmitri now confronts the one thing that the Grand Inquisitor says man abhors most: a free choice. He can either escape with Grushenka to America or suffer in Siberia for a crime of which he is innocent.

Ivan's Guilt

Chapters Five through Eight are a study in the psychology of guilt. For the past two months Ivan has struggled to keep his own responsibility in his father's death repressed in the unconscious. Now the first cracks appear in the walls of his defenses. When he finally, at the end of Chapter Eight, recognizes the magnitude of his guilt, he sinks into madness. In these chapters, Ivan's behavior is motivated exclusively by his desire to clear himself of any moral responsibility for the crime. This is a particularly difficult enterprise since he never concealed his hatred for Fyodor, and on several occasions hinted in subtle ways that he wished his father dead. Now there is evidence that perhaps Smerdyakov committed the crime under the influence of Ivan's ideas. If this is so, then Ivan is morally just as guilty as the real murderer.

Ivan's moral responsibility hinges upon the answer to four crucial questions: Did Smerdyakov understand that Ivan wanted his father's death; second, did he give Smerdyakov his tacit consent to kill Fyodor by going to Moscow; next, what did Smerdyakov imply when he insisted that he could sham epileptic seizures; and finally, who actually committed the murder? While on the surface Ivan appears to expend considerable effort in search of the facts, on a deeper level he frantically does all he can to obscure the truth. Smerdyakov senses this immediately when his brother visits him for the first time in the hospital.

Smerdyakov, it turns out, is a good deal cleverer than anyone thought. Explaining the significance of Chermashnaya, he says that he urged Ivan to go there not only to get out of harm's way but also because Moscow is further away and Ivan would be unable to return in time to save him from Dmitri's wrath. As to the shamming of fits, Smerdyakov assures him that he was merely boasting: "It was just foolishness. I liked you so much then, and was openhearted with you." Finally, he delivers such a well-thought-out and coherent analysis of the circumstantial evidence pointing to his own innocence that Ivan feels reassured. Significantly, he leaves the hospital without asking the most important question of all: did Smerdyakov know that Ivan wanted Fyodor's death? Still, Ivan receives an indirect answer in Smerdyakov's response to Ivan's statement that he would say nothing about his brother's ability to sham fits: "And if you don't speak of that, I shall say nothing of that conversation of ours at the gate." Although his conscious mind notices nothing, his unconscious registers the true meaning of that statement and it begins to prey upon his mind.

For two weeks Ivan almost seems to forget his indirect involvement in Fyodor's death. But then he begins to be haunted by several questions. Why on his last night in his father's house had he crept out onto the staircase and listened to what the old man was doing? Why had he been so depressed on the journey next day? And finally, why did he keep telling himself in Moscow "I am a scoundrel." As these thoughts are going through his mind, he meets Alyosha in the street. Ivan reminds him of that evening when Dmitri burst in and beat Fyodor, after which Ivan had remarked that "one reptile devours another." Ivan now

BRIGHT NOTES STUDY GUIDE

asks: "Tell me, did you think then that I desired father's death or not.... Didn't you fancy then that what I wished for was just ... that Dmitri should kill father, and as soon as possible, ... and that I myself was even prepared to help bring that about?" Alyosha's affirmative answer confirms Ivan's worst fears, for if Alyosha could discern his wish, then it was quite likely that Smerdyakov could have sensed it too. Ivan decides to visit Smerdyakov again to clear up this matter.

Smerdyakov tells Ivan the truth during the second and third visits because he wrongly suspects Ivan is trying to blame to save his own skin. His former admiration for Ivan is transformed into malignant hatred. Smerdyakov tells him that he committed the crime because he knew Ivan wanted him to and that his departure for Moscow was a clear signal to proceed: "So that it was just by that more than anything you showed me what was in your mind." Smerdyakov goes on to say that he has a clear conscience because even though he killed him, it was in accordance with Ivan's express desire. He even provided him with the philosophical justification: "You murdered him; you are the real murderer, I was only your instrument, your faithful servant, and it was following your words I did it." Subsequently, he tells Ivan in detail how he committed the crime and ends by producing the stolen money. Following this grueling revelation Ivan returns home where he experiences the first symptoms of madness in the form of a hallucination. Before examining these conversations with the Devil, we must first consider both Ivan's and Smerdyakov's attitude to the crime.

Nature Of Evil

Ivan's and Smerdyakov's reaction to the crime raises several metaphysical problems. As we have seen, Ivan unwittingly provides Smerdyakov with the philosophical justification for crime: "If God doesn't exist, then everything is lawful." This statement can also be rephrased to read: "If you don't believe in God, then you're free to do anything you can get away with," (Ivan's idea is one of the chief structural principles of Joseph Heller's *Catch-22*.) When Ivan sees how his idea is degraded into a moral sanction for swindling and crime, he is overwhelmed with guilt and his personality begins to disintegrate. It appears as if he lacked the inner strength either to live according to his own values or to accept the responsibility for his actions. The man who extolled the virtues of free will, believed in self-sufficiency, and wrote "The Legend of the Grand Inquisitor" acts like a moral coward. Smerdyakov, by contrast, has killed with impunity, and at least from his point of view has done society a favor. He is confident, in full possession of his self-respect, and has a clear conscience. He is even looking forward to spending the money.

Why, then, does Dostoyevsky approve of Ivan and make him his hero? Why, even though he falls into madness, does the author hold out the hope of his recovery? And for what reason does Smerdyakov, apparently the stronger, commit suicide; a fate that the author reserves only for such hopeless cases as Svidrigaylov and Stavrogin? To answer these questions we must examine them in the light of Dostoyevsky's conception of evil.

When writing this novel, Dostoyevsky struggled with the problem that has occupied Christian philosophers since St. Augustine. How can one explain the existence of evil? If God is the creator of all things, and if God is good then how is it possible for evil to exist in a world created by an infinitely good God? The problem in understanding evil is that we tend to think of it as something which exists. As defined by St. Augustine and presented by Dostoyevsky in this novel, evil is not positive thing, a created entity, rather it signifies the privation of something. Evil exists only as an absence, the absence of God. Or in different terms, evil is where good is not.

In the light of this definition let us take another look at Smerdyakov. This man is evil not because he has made a decision to be so, but because in excluding God from his life, he has extinguished within himself the living sense of the good. Having no conception of good and evil, he is able to regard all human action, including murder, as one and the same. The author only appears to say that in freeing himself from God, a person can liberate himself from guilt and so find a new source of strength. On the contrary, he demonstrates that if a person can cope with crime it means that God is absent from him. Of course, Smerdyakov is not strong. As we have already seen, he is vain and lacks courage. He is terrified Dmitri might kill him, and breaks into tears when Ivan strikes him on the shoulder during their second interview.

Another problem closely related to these ideas is the question of man's free will. Dostoyevsky believed that although God has foreknowledge of man's actions, man still is free to make his own decisions. The contradiction may be resolved with a modern explanation of St. Augustine's ideas on the subject.

Suppose that a person were sitting atop a hill watching a highway leading to the top. Two cars approach from opposite directions at high speed, their view of each other blocked by the hill. From where the man sits, he knows that a collision will occur, yet his knowledge of the inevitable does not cause the collision. God sees our lives in much the same way. He knows that whatever collisions await us are the result of our past free choices. If we make the right choices, there will be no "collisions."

God will be with us and we will be saved because the concept of grace allows God to interfere.

This brings us to the most important point of Dostoyevsky's ideas about the way God works in everyday human activity. If a person denies God, he puts himself outside His jurisprudence. In this state of self-sufficiency his unguided will tends to make the wrong decisions. If God is present within him, he will eventually will the right things and be saved through the grace of God.

We are now able to conclude that Ivan's intense guilt-feelings are not a sign of weakness at all, but signify the presence of God within him. It is this that makes him accept responsibility for a crime of which he is legally innocent, and then drives him to confess his guilt at the trial despite his knowledge that to do so will ruin him. And even though he goes insane, the author tells us that his condition is not hopeless and that there may be new life for him. His present weakness will be a future source of strength.

Ivan's Devil

During the course of the novel each of the three brothers has a dream or vision which engenders a spiritual rebirth in them. When Alyosha begins to rebel against God, his faith is restored by the dream of Jesus' miracle at the wedding feast. Dmitri's dream of the starving babe and the burned-out village teaches him the value of suffering and shows him what he must do to redeem his past life. Ivan's transforming vision is a conversation with the Devil. It is a kind of internal odyssey of self-discovery that strips away the false conceptions he has of himself and teaches him the necessity of accepting himself as he really is. Although the Devil is presented as a real person, the reader soon realizes that he is a hallucination.

Ivan imagines the Devil in the form of disgusting snob. He poses as a sophisticated liberal who has read a few books and so considers himself well informed on a number of subjects but who, in fact, is a pseudo-intellectual of the 1860s. He looks as if he at one time belonged to good society, but had, after a carefree and spendthrift youth, been impoverished by the abolition of serfdom. Finding himself in the role of a poor relation, he now wanders from one good friend to another accommodating himself in exchange for a few months' room and board. The manner in which he dresses reflects the shallowness of his ideas. His clothes are well made and of good quality, but on closer scrutiny are seen to be out of fashion, shiny from wear, and slightly soiled. He gives every appearance of gentility on a small budget, an impecunious friend who wants to please. Under this guise he tortures Ivan mercilessly by dragging his most cherished ideas about God and the human condition down to his level of banality.

This **episode** should be regarded in a positive way because it helps Ivan, for the first time, to examine his ideas from a new perspective. Not surprisingly, he is appalled by the hypocrisy of his beliefs. First, the Devil shows him that he believes in God after all and that intellectual pride had prevented him from admitting the existence of such a belief. In fact, his atheism and utopian theories for the improvement of mankind are manifestations of his intrinsic faith. And he finally sees that it was pride and arrogance that gave birth to his doctrine of man-godhood. "Destroy the idea of God in man," as Ivan is fond of saying, "and the old conception of the universe will fall of itself." Ivan always claimed that ultimately out of this destruction the man-god will appear. Self-reliant, serene, and no longer wasting his time over a non-existent after-life, he will devote himself to making the world a better place to live in. If there is no more God and no more immortality, then "all things are lawful." But as the Devil dramatically demonstrates, such an idea merely becomes a moral sanction for crime when placed in the hands of unprincipled men.

This **episode** of self-discovery reaches its peak when Alyosha arrives to inform Ivan that Smerdyakov has committed suicide. Alyosha finds his brother very excited, nearly delirious, because he is ready to perform an act entirely out of keeping with his self-image. Ivan is struggling with an overpowering desire to go to Dmitri's trial and confess that he is the true murderer because he encouraged Smerdyakov to kill his father. This he knows to be a virtuous act. It upsets him because he never had believed in virtue, considering it a pernicious quality arising from the belief in God. He also experiences other feelings which until now he had regarded as values of the unenlightened herd. He longs for praise as a reward for his integrity. He fancies himself as someone who will tell the truth no matter what the consequences. And even though he knows that his confession will be greeted with disbelief, he also knows that he will go anyway out of a new found sense of principle. In short, the great discovery that Ivan makes about himself, that wounds his pride to the quick and negates all his former life as well as everything he stands for and believes in, is that he is a Christian and has always been one. As the truth about himself dawns for the first time and he perceives the hypocrisy of his life and the extent of his intellectual dishonesty, he is overwhelmed and passes out.

This experience shows Ivan that if he is to live at peace with himself and with the world, he must learn to accept his condition, recognize and accept himself for what he really is. Above all, he must cease trying to live a life without Christ.

BOOK XII

Trial

Dmitri's trial is not a study in jurisprudence but, as the title of this Book - "A Judicial Error" -suggests, a spectacle that has been arranged for the town's entertainment. The case has become known all over Russia and people, especially lawyers, journey all the way from Petersburg, Moscow, and beyond to watch the proceedings. Lawyers come to study the skill and brilliant legal tactics of the celebrated defense attorney from Petersburg, Fetyukovitch, while the ladies are simply attracted by Dmitri's reputation as a lady's man.

The arrangements for the trial indicate its importance. A row of comfy chairs is placed behind the three judges to accommodate the important personages, one section is set aside for the lawyers, and the balcony is turned over to the spectators. The gory evidence, consisting of the blood-soaked clothes and the brass pestle, is placed conspicuously in the middle of the room and naturally becomes the center of attention. As Ivan rightly remarks, everyone pretends horror at the brutal crime but what really attracts them are the gruesome details of the murder. The spectators come to be pleasantly horrified: "If there hadn't been a murder, they'd have been angry and gone home ill-humored."

Tactics

How the two lawyers regard the case is evident from the outset. The prosecutor looks upon the trial as an opportunity to enhance his reputation as a brilliant attorney and so increase his chances of getting out of the provinces. Fetyukovitch, too, is not blind to the case's fringe benefits. He has made an enviable reputation for himself by defending and often winning seemingly hopeless but celebrated cases in the provinces.

Dmitri's case is particularly difficult because there is no material evidence in his favor. So Fetyukovitch employs the efficient tactic of besmirching the character of the witnesses for the prosecution in order to discredit their testimony. Accordingly, he points out that Grigory was drunk on vodka when he saw the open garden-gate and likely did not know what he saw the night of the murder. After Rakitin's brilliant speech, Fetyukovitch reveals that not only did Grushenka bribe him to bring Alyosha to her apartment, but also that she is his cousin. This revelation comes as a complete surprise to the audience, humiliates the young man, and renders his testimony suspect. Likewise, Trifon Borisovitch, the owner of the tavern in Mokroe, and the two Poles are discredited in that Fetyukovitch proves that the former stole a hundred rubles from Dmitri and that the latter cheated at cards. Despite his adroitness and skill, Dmitri's attorney does not succeed in turning up new facts; they come by themselves.

Katerina's Testimony

Katerina testifies twice. The first time she tells the truth, the second time she gives full expression to her hatred and lies. In the first testimony she relates the circumstances of her relationship to Dmitri and tells the court how she went to Dmitri for the money to save her father and how he bowed to her and asked nothing in return. Such frankness and self-sacrifice despite the gossip that is bound to follow creates a strong impression in Dmitri's favor. This could have been the end of the matter but for Ivan's subsequent testimony.

Suddenly, Ivan interrupts the court to announce that Smerdyakov is the guilty party and he then produces three thousand rubles to prove it. He concludes his presentation with the remark: "He [Smerdyakov] murdered him and I incited him to do it ... Who doesn't desire his father's death?" After this avowal Ivan suffers a final attack of brain fever. He begins shouting incoherently, talks about the Devil, flings an usher to the floor, and has to be carried out by force. This spectacle has a profound effect on Katerina and precipitates her fit of hysteria.

Ivan's act of self-immolation brings to the surface Katerina's secret love for him and her hatred for Dmitri whom she only thinks she loves. Unable to bear the prospect that the man whom she truly loves is destroying himself for the man she hates, she loses her self-control. She produces the letter in which Dmitri announces he will get the three thousand he owes her even if he has "to kill his father."

This is Katerina's great moment of revenge. Now she can pay Dmitri back for his bow to her on that night, for his faithlessness with Grushenka that wounded her heart and for which she cannot forgive him. At last it is revealed that she had always wrongly believed that Dmitri was laughing at her and despising her for offering her body in exchange for money to save her father. She is firmly convinced that Dmitri looks upon her as a base creature. Consequently, her love for him is a "hysterical, 'lacerated' love only from pride, from wounded pride, and that love was not like love, but more like revenge."

Katerina's emotional outburst is followed by a new attack of hysteria brought on by intense shame. She falls sobbing and writhing to the floor and is carried out.

Prosecutor's Speech

Ippolit Kirillovitch regards his final address to the jury as the pinnacle of his career. Furthermore, it serves as an opportunity to display his liberal and progressive views on jurisprudence in particular and on the course of human civilization in general.

The prosecutor's first statements deal with the lack of moral principle in Russia and the fact that such crimes as parricide no longer horrify. It is high time that Russian society look at itself. The Karamazovs provide a good opportunity to do so because this family represents a cross-section of modern Russia. Fyodor is a depraved profligate whose life revolves about the satiation of his senses. He has failed as a father and as a human being. Ivan represents the highly educated intelligentsia who have lost faith in everything, believe in nothing, and who infect the lower classes with ideas too advanced for their own good. Alyosha personifies the spiritual dimension of Russia. He is devout, seeks to remain close to the basic principles of society, and rejects Western intellectualism. Dmitri is Russia as she is. He is characterized by that peculiar Russian capacity for "broadness," the ability to combine the most incongruous contradictions within himself. He is noble and base, self-sacrificing and selfish, spiritual and sensual, all at the same time.

The prosecutor's tactics consist in psychologically interpreting Dmitri's every action between his arrival in town and his arrest. We may cite the analysis of Dmitri's story about the fifteen hundred rubles which he carried in a bag tied round his neck as characteristic of this approach. Dmitri claims that he spent only half of Katerina's money because as long as he had that other half he could always give it back to her saying that he might be a scoundrel, but not a thief. Ippolit calls this a "marvellous explanation." More likely, he says, Dmitri would have acted like any normal person who needed money. At the first excuse he would have unpicked the bag, taken out a hundred rubles and spent it. Then a few days later he would have taken out another hundred and so on until there were only a hundred left. Since that was hardly worth returning, he then would have spent that too.

The prosecutor then examines Smerdyakov as a possible suspect and "proves" that he could not have possibly committed the crime because of his character. He had the "heart of a chicken" and the "soul of a dog." He was terrified of his own shadow while his mind was weakened by epilepsy. And again, if Smerdyakov really did confess the crime to Ivan, why did Ivan not inform the authorities immediately instead of waiting until the next morning when he had an attack of brain fever? As to the three thousand rubles which Ivan says he got from Smerdyakov, it is likely his own money because the prosecutor knows that he received a large sum by mail a few days earlier. The prosecutor even interprets Dmitri's jumping down from the wall to see after Grigory as no more than an effort to make sure the only witness was dead.

Finally, he concludes the speech with an emotional appeal to the jury's patriotism. Russia is like a troika racing full tilt towards destruction while other nations stand aside in disgust and horror. It is the jury's duty to find Dmitri guilty to show Europe that Russia is not two steps this side of barbarism after all, that even here parricide is punished.

The fundamental error in the Prosecutor's speech is that he makes the facts fit a preconceived conclusion. This is like trying to solve a mathematical problem backwards from the answer.

Furthermore, psychology is a specious form of reasoning that can be used to prove anything, as the counsel for the defense quickly points out.

Speech For The Defense

The first part of Fetyukovitch's speech is a refutation of the charges. While admitting to an overwhelming chain of circumstantial evidence, he says that not one of the facts can stand criticism if examined individually. Moreover, he criticizes the prosecutor's use of the psychological method because that is "a knife that cuts both ways." For instance, at one point the prosecutor asserted that Dmitri evinced total lack of caution in leaving the torn envelope on the floor, an oversight typical of an amateur in a hurry. Yet in the next sentence he looks upon Dmitri's going back to see if Grigory were alive as the act of a calculating, cold-blooded killer. If so, then why wipe the victim's blood with a handkerchief that could be used as evidence, and why leave the weapon behind as "evidence"? In this way Fetyukovitch refutes all the evidence and shows how the prosecution has made the facts fit a preconceived conclusion.

Fetyukovitch is the only one in the novel who comes near understanding how the murder took place, who did it, and why. His deductions are based primarily on his interview with Smerdyakov. In Smerdyakov he did not find a weak and timorous man, but one of considerable intelligence and resourcefulness. These qualities, however, were poisoned by envy and vindictiveness brought on by wounded vanity. He was ashamed of his parentage and he intensely resented his position in comparison with that of his legitimate brothers. They had all the rights, the inheritance, and position while he had nothing and was the cook. Then one day he watches Fyodor squander three thousand rubles on his passion for Grushenka. This money would have made his career, it would have enabled him to leave Russia and live in France as a Frenchman. No wonder he contemplated parricide.

Fetyukovitch's best argument is on the nature of parricide. The word means to kill one's father. But what, he asks, constitutes fatherhood? Does the mere act of begetting mean that a man should be honored and obeyed? Can a person be called father if he neglects his child, tries to cheat him of his inheritance, and get him locked up for not paying his debts? It is an absurdity, he says, to call Fyodor a father simply because he happens to be the same flesh and blood. True fatherhood is something that is earned. It implies a sense of responsibility for his children and concern for their welfare. Fetyukovitch's logic is impeccable. Since Fyodor is not a father in the true sense of the word, then his murder is not a true case of parricide.

Fetyukovitch's final appeal sounds like a summation of Dostoyevsky's own views on the nature of crime and punishment. If the jury condemns Dmitri they will only succeed in easing the criminal's conscience and in making him feel justified. It will result in his proclaiming that: "I owe them nothing now, and owe no one anything for ever. They are wicked and I will be wicked. They are cruel and I will be cruel."

If the jury really wants to punish him in the most fearful and awful way, then it should show him love and mercy. The only effective punishment consists in the criminal's recognition of his own guilt and the anguish of conscience that follows. And again, it should be kept in mind that the court does not exist solely to punish but also to work for the criminal's salvation. To do this the court must remove any cause for later vindictiveness. Then: "With tears of penitence and poignant, tender anguish, he will exclaim: 'Others are better than I, they wanted to save me, not to ruin me!'" The jury will then have brought about the criminal's rehabilitation.

Verdict

The jury proves to be immune to all the rhetoric and emotionalism. Dmitri is guilty on every count. The verdict is brutal, final, and without qualification. It appears as if everything that went on during the trial was pointless, or perhaps even unheard. The jury cannot even be commended for adhering to the facts because they have ignored the facts and condemned an innocent man. Or have they? We may well ask what Dostoyevsky wants to tell the reader. He is doing two things. First, he is criticizing the legal system and second, he is showing how the peasant's verdict transcends the legal process.

Considering the first point, it is clear that the legal process does not reveal the facts but obscures them. The truth is ridiculed and the lies are believed with eagerness. Katerina's confession is false and accepted while Ivan's confession is true and laughed at. The court permits the ambitious and unprincipled Rakitin a disquisition on politics and morality but the innocent Dmitri must shout and pound the table to be heard. The trial is little more than an exercise in rhetoric, intellectual exhibitionism, and character assassination. In order to understand this attack upon the legal system, we must recall what the author thought about reason.

Among Dostoyevsky's major themes, from *Notes from Underground* to *The Brothers Karamazov*, is the nature of reason. He was fond of showing that reason is a purely cerebral process that can be made to serve any master. Its chief weakness is that it excludes the validity of feeling and intuition as a basis for decision-making. Dostoyevsky believed that for any action to be human, it must encompass all aspects of the personality. The legal process prevailing in Russia at that time and in the United States today rigorously excludes feeling, intuition, or emotion. We can better illustrate Dostoyevsky's point by recalling a celebrated court case of the mid-1970s. A young woman took an overdose of amphetamines which injured her brain and put her into a permanent coma. Her parents petitioned the court to disconnect the life-sustaining machine, arguing that their daughter had degenerated into a vegetable and that letting her die was the humane thing to do. The judge categorically refused to visit the invalid before making a decision, insisting that he could not permit his decision to be influenced by "emotion." Likewise, Fetyukovitch's conclusions are rejected because they are based on intuition and feeling.

So reason triumphs over feeling. But it is a hollow victory because the reasoners lose on the human level. Rakitin is humiliated before the court and Fetyukovitch wins the approval of the audience and the legal experts for which Ippolit thirsted. Most important of all, the legal process has made a mockery of the law, court decorum, and fair play. Dostoyevsky's message, then, is a simple one. Until the law is humanized by taking account of feeling, it will continue to be inhuman.

There is still the matter of the jury's verdict. Why is an innocent man found guilty? This problem becomes more complicated when we remember that the author believed in peasants and looked upon them as the true representatives of the Russian spirit. Unlike the intelligentsia which had lost contact with primary values and whose judgment was influenced by literature, philosophy, and ideas from the West. The uneducated peasant, at least from the author's point of view, basically acts according to Christian principles. At the same time Dostoyevsky approves of Dmitri. Despite his erring ways, he has not lost sight of the good and loves his fellow man. Since Dostoyevsky has a high opinion of the peasants and an equally high opinion of Dmitri, how do we reconcile their verdict with his innocence? Because in a broader sense, Dmitri is guilty. The author's conception of guilt supports this conclusion.

In the section on the Nature Of Suffering we pointed out that the Ten Commandments are concerned chiefly with actions whereas Christ's law focuses on feeling. If action is subordinated to feeling, the concept of sin and guilt undergoes a basic change. What a person thought was much more important to Christ than how he acted. He said that thinking about killing someone or dreaming of seducing another's spouse amounts to the same as doing it. In this sense Dmitri is guilty because not only did he hate his father and desire his death, his entire life was corrupted by the spirit of the Karamazovs. Dmitri has an idea of what is on the jury's mind when he says: "I was erring, but I loved what is good. Every instant I strove to reform, but I lived like a wild beast." So the jury goes to the heart of the problem and judges him both for his profligate, Karamazov way of life and for desiring his father's death. Legally he is innocent, but morally he is guilty.

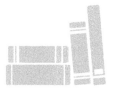

THE BROTHERS KARAMAZOV

EPILOGUE

The first chapter of the "Epilog" is a deft little study in the psychology of guilt. Katerina's conscience tortures her for betraying Dmitri at the trial. The pain is intensified because a loss of self-respect has followed the acquisition of self-knowledge. She now sees how her hatred masqueraded as love, how revenge festered beneath external forgiveness. Perceiving for the first time how hatred motivates her life, seeing the magnitude of her hypocrisy, and understanding that she brought this misery on herself, she aches to confess it all to Alyosha "with tears and cries and hysterical writings on the floor." In maliciously perjuring herself and thus sending an innocent man to twenty years' penal servitude, she has transgressed one of those inner absolutes which result in disintegration of the personality. In such a state the transgressor finds it impossible to forgive himself.

It is in search of this forgiveness that she visits Dmitri in prison. But instead of admitting to herself that she wants, even needs, to ask his pardon, she regards the confrontation as an opportunity to punish herself. No matter that a few honest words pass between them during the meeting. She deludes herself to the end. When Grushenka comes in she asks her forgiveness, knowing but not caring that everyone sees through the lie.

Dmitri feels equally guilty about Katerina. Only after she breaks down at the trial does he understand how grievously he wounded her. Truly remorseful, he then asks her forgiveness and offers his own. This done, he can leave for Siberia.

Yet Dmitri is not going to Siberia. At one point he looked forward to the hardship and suffering in store for him as a means of redeeming his past life. But since Grushenka cannot come with him, and since as an innocent man his character could not endure the personal abuse, he has decided to accept another kind of punishment more commensurate with his guilt. He will escape to America where he and Grushenka will work the land and suffer homesickness. (Dostoyevsky regarded exile as the worst possible punishment for a true Russian. By the same token, a native who voluntarily lived outside Russia was not a Russian.) After a few years they would return home and live quietly somewhere in the South.

Alyosha approves of this plan because he knows that Dmitri is not a man to carry that kind of a burden: "Listen, you are not ready, and such a cross is not for you. You wanted to make yourself another man by suffering. I say, only remember that other man always, all your life and wherever you go, and that will be enough for you. Your refusal of that great cross will only serve to make you feel all your life an even greater duty, and that constant feeling will do more to make you a new man, perhaps, than if you went there."

Alyosha as Christ Figure

This quotation also tells us a great deal about the development of Alyosha's character and his role in the book. At the beginning of the novel we see him as a timid young man, reticent, and unsure of himself. But as he becomes more and more involved with people, he matures rapidly until in the "Epilog" he has become the dominant figure. He tells Katerina that she "ought" to visit Dmitri and when she hesitates, he virtually orders her to go. He "allows" Dmitri to forego his official punishment and escape to America. He forbids the guards to let Rakitin visit his brother and, most surprising, he is even planning to break the law by bribing an official to let Dmitri go.

But Alyosha's greatest success is with the boys. By this time he has been completely accepted as their spiritual leader. Once again he takes on the aspects of a Christ figure gathering disciples about him before beginning his ministry. Like Christ speaking to the people, Alyosha delivers a "sermon at the stone" in which he reveals his gospel of love and kindness in dealing with the world. Like Christ, he holds out the promise of a Hereafter: "Certainly we shall rise again, certainly we shall see each other and shall tell each other with joy and gladness all that has happened."

The novel ends with all the boys shouting: "Hurrah for Karamazov."

THE BROTHERS KARAMAZOV

. . . .

Alyosha

Several times in the text we have mentioned that Alyosha functions as a Christ figure. If we isolate the specific motifs of his life and compare them to those of Christ, we will be able to identify the principle underlying his role in the book.

Jesus' life consisted of a series of traditionally associated motifs: preparation for His mission, temptation, excursion into the world to fulfill His mission, gathering of disciples, performing of various miracles, and proclaiming a new way of life. Dostoyevsky transfigured all of these motifs in Alyosha, leaving for an unwritten sequel the remaining motifs: a last supper, lonely agony, betrayal, trial, and crucifixion.

The first motif occurs soon after Alyosha arrives in town when he comes under the influence of Father Zossima. Zossima prepares him for his mission in the world. He teaches Alyosha that Christianity is a religion of joy and happiness and instructs him in the doctrine "all are responsible for all." The Elder tells him that if people make love the organizing principle of their lives not only will they understand the divine scheme of things but all the misery of humanity will be alleviated. Finally, he orders Alyosha to leave the monastery and "sojourn in the world" immediately after his death because Alyosha has the power to ease the suffering of humanity.

Alyosha's first hesitating steps into the world are met by an onrush of disturbing and disintegrating influences which threaten to overwhelm him. His temptation is initiated by Rakitin, a kind of intellectual Satan. Rakitin takes him to see Grushenka, expecting that she will trigger the Karamazov sensuality in him. But at the crucial moment Alyosha's compassion for Grushenka's suffering brings out her better qualities and she abandons the idea. That same night Alyosha undergoes an experience which in its effect resembles a baptism. Praying by Zossima's coffin he has a vision of Christ. It provides him with a deeper understanding of Christianity and launches him upon his mission in the world.

Immediately after this experience, Alyosha becomes involved with a group of school boys. Through his personal charm he breaks down the boys' defenses and they soon gather round him like disciples. He teaches them his creed of love and kindness, develops their conscience, and succeeds in completely transforming them. His greatest success is with Kolya Krassotkin, a potential Simon Peter. Precocious, self-confident, and a natural leader, at thirteen he is already an embryonic nihilist. But under Alyosha's influence, he becomes the chief force in transforming the hatred between Ilusha and the other boys into a sense of brotherhood.

While Alyosha turns no stones into bread, he accomplishes several acts of healing which are miracles in their implication. Through kindness, the force of his personality, and through an uncanny skill in the psychological assessment of others, he heals

Grushenka's hatred of the world, he turns the enmity between Ilusha and the other boys into love, forces Katerina to face the true nature of her feelings toward Dmitri, and gives the crippled Lise and the convicted Dmitri hope for a new life. Finally, through the unspoken example of his own life, he shows Ivan that universal happiness can be brought about if man organizes his life according to the best principles of Christianity.

Dmitri

In Dmitri, Dostoyevsky personifies one of the many extremes of which man is capable. What Ivan is to intellect and Alyosha to spirituality, Dmitri is to sensuality. Dmitri expresses himself and finds fulfillment as a human being through his senses. The exhilaration that he finds in passion and wild living is no less intense than Ivan's pleasure in working out a difficult problem in aesthetics.

In Dmitri, however, the sensual impulse is carried to excess, and he becomes its prisoner. Until later in the novel he is unable and unwilling to exist in any other fashion. Not an occasional lover of debauchery, he looks for it, seeks it out, and consciously reminds himself to act in the most depraved way. He tells a story about exploring a young girl's body on a midnight sleigh ride and then, instead of marrying her as she expected, he stayed away, sensuously enjoying her pain from a distance. When he organizes a drinking party it invariably develops into a drunken orgy with too much wine and kinky sex. He brawls, fights duels, and positively enjoys the profligate's life. Ironically, trouble begins the first time he acts nobly.

When Katerina comes to offer her body in exchange for enough money to save her father, Dmitri prefers to humiliate her by giving her the money with a bow. Immediately thereafter, she dedicates her life to saving Dmitri from himself. But Dmitri does not want to be saved. Life with Katerina means a superficial, lukewarm existence in which anger is permitted, but not rage; love, but not passion; happiness, but not ecstasy. So he breaks the engagement when he meets Gruschenka, whose highly sensuous nature more closely resembles his own. The purity of Dmitri's love overcomes the impulse to degradation. He struggles to break free of the Karamazov spirit so that he can lead a tranquil life with Grushenka. It is this which makes him curse his debauchery, grieve over the way he treated Katerina, and look upon the suffering in store for him as an opportunity to both destroy and redeem his past.

Fyodor

This person illustrates what can happen to a human being who excludes the spiritual from his life and dedicates himself exclusively to the cultivation of sensual pleasure. The motivating force in his life is "the spirit of the Karamazov's," a kind of primal urge which calls upon the individual to abandon civilized behavior in favor of its polar opposite. He positively loves vice, corruption, and sensual delights of every kind. Yet he degrades sensuality. To him love is lust, sex is lasciviousness, and alcohol an instrument of depravity.

Accordingly, Fyodor is a poor father who regards his children as an annoying hindrance to his way of life. He cheats Dmitri of his inheritance, buys up all his debts, and then tries to get him locked up for not paying them. He offers his son's mistress, Grushenka, money to spend the night with him and then chuckles over Dmitri's insane jealousy.

For his other two sons, he presents a mockery of everything they believe in and tells disgraceful stories about the way he made love to their mother. He has no sense of propriety or decency, and no self-control where matters of the flesh are concerned.

Fyodor's public life reflects his inner decay. He spent several years with Jews in Odessa mastering the fine points of Machiavellian finance and returns to town to open several taverns. He lends money at outrageous interest, forecloses at the first opportunity, and succeeds in amassing a considerable fortune which he then dedicates to his lust.

He knows that both the townspeople and his sons (except Alyosha) disrespect him. Yet, the more society condemns him, the more he plays the buffoon. The more society is shocked by his behavior, the more perverted he becomes. And he knows the reason he acts in this way, but instead of trying to improve himself, he seeks further degradation.

It is now clear why Fyodor bears the chief responsibility for his own death. Just before the murder he is abandoned by everyone in a position to help him. As if by an unspoken agreement Ivan leaves for Moscow, Alyosha stays at the monastery, and Grigory drinks too much vodka. Smerdyakov, it seems, is merely acting in accordance with the general desire.

Grushenka

Highly intelligent, self-assured, and strong, Grushenka impresses the reader as strikingly modern. She is devoid of those characteristics which are traditionally associated with femininity. She knows who she is, what she stands for, and how to get what she wants out of life. Possessing a keen sense of business and a capacity for hard work, she amasses a small fortune which enables her to buy her freedom from the merchant Samsonov.

Grushenka's liberation from the stereotype is more apparent when compared to such characters as Mme. Hohlakov and the ladies of the local society whose lives appear to revolve about gossip, the forthcoming governor's ball, and what they are going to wear the next day. They lose themselves in motherhood and willingly subordinate themselves to the concept Kirche, Kinder, Kuche. Hence they are shallow and tiresome.

What we learn from the study of Dostoyevsky is that he makes no rigid distinctions between male and female psychology. Most of his female **protagonists** are portrayed as strong, self-reliant, and determined to arrange their lives to suit themselves. They are just as tortured, cruel, and sadistic, or as loving, gentle, and idealistic as his men. In Dostoyevsky's world there is no such thing as typically feminine behavior any more than there is a typically masculine one. The author knew that a person's behavior is determined largely by the requirements of cultural role-playing. Behavior and character development arise from the circumstances in which the **protagonists** find themselves and not from any a priori absolutes.

Ivan

Well-educated and endowed with penetrating insight, Ivan represents the type of person who views himself as wholly independent and free to determine his own destiny. He rejects all ethical standards not his own and sees human society as brutal, futile, and disordered. He believes that an ultimate reality exists. And he wants to get at it. He is confident that rational insight into the ordering of the universe will provide the key for bringing about a better world. As a result, reason and intellect replace emotion and intuition as the faculties by which a man may apprehend the scheme of things.

Ivan's experience with suffering humanity leads him to search for a better social order. First, the Christian interpretation of things must be done away with and the idea of God destroyed because He has bungled in making happiness, fulfillment, and salvation too hard and illogical. Ivan's reasoning is impeccable. If man does not believe in God, then he will no longer fear losing his immortal soul. He will then be free to create a new order upon the ashes of the old. Ivan formulates his idea in the phrase: "If God doesn't exist, then everything is lawful," by which he also means that everything is possible. It will then be possible to prevent war, starvation, and alleviate the sufferings of mankind in general. Ivan assumes that if humanity is freed from the tyranny of the Ten Commandments, man's reason will automatically tell him what is right.

While Dostoyevsky was sympathetic with Ivan's desire to improve man's lot, he believed that universal happiness cannot be achieved by imposing a transcendental harmony on the world. Furthermore, the rationalist view of man is arbitrary and one-dimensional. In ignoring the emotional-intuitive side of man, he fails to realize that nature, love, God and the soul have validity only through feeling.

Ivan's fate is the author's way of showing what he believed to be the basic fallacy in ordering one's life exclusively according to the dictates of reason. When Ivan arrives in town he takes an interest in Smerdyakov, tells him about his ideas, and explains his theory "if God doesn't exist, then everything is lawful," But

Smerdyakov understands it as "If God is dead, then you're free to do anything you can get away with." Set free from the restraining influence of religion, he kills his father in cold blood. When Ivan realizes that he is primarily responsible for the crime in that he provided Smerdyakov with the philosophical justification and gave his unspoken consent, he is overwhelmed by guilt.

The experience of guilt where his theory says there should be none proves false all his ideas about the supremacy of reason, spiritual self-sufficiency, and man-godhood. It is not Fyodor's death that shatters him, but the invalidity of his theory and the realization that his true values are Christian. No matter what his reason tells him, these values are cultural absolutes and cannot be transgressed with impunity. His illness is his punishment.

Yet Dostoyevsky holds out the hope of Ivan's recovery. The fact that he confesses his guilt at the trial and that he is struggling to acknowledge the truth about himself indicates that traditional Christian principles have not been extinguished in him. Therein lies his salvation.

Katerina

In Dostoyevsky's pantheon of unforgivable sins, pride ranks just after atheism. Pride is the motivating force of Katerina's life, gives birth to her hatred, her masochism, and her thirst for revenge.

When Dmitri first meets her, she refuses even to look at him, having been informed of his unsavory reputation. Whenever they happen to meet socially, she greets him with the cool arrogance which the aristocracy reserves only for those infinitely below them. Then suddenly she is confronted with the necessity of offering her body to him in exchange for enough money to rescue her father's reputation. When she comes for the money, Dmitri quickly sees that if he is to gain a victory over her and humiliate her beyond endurance, then his actions must exceed hers in nobility. So he gives her the money for nothing and even includes a bow. Unknown to Dmitri, this deed wounds Katerina's pride to the quick and she will stop at nothing to even the score.

To repay the insult, Katerina must make an even greater sacrifice: herself. She will marry Dmitri, reform him, and rededicate him to a productive life. Yet as the story unfolds, it is clear that she has no genuine affection for him, nor is she interested in reforming him. Her "love" is a love of her own suffering. The more he insults her, the more she likes it, and the more she loves him. She does not want him to change. She loves him precisely because he insults her. If Dmitri reformed, she would cease caring about him. She needs Dmitri's humiliation to admire her own nobility. For it is only by constantly forgiving Dmitri for his insults and faithlessness that she can at last prove herself the nobler person after all.

But as it happens, Dmitri does not want to be forgiven. He enjoys "the filthy back alleys and the she devil." Katerina knows that as long as Dmitri does not need her, she never be able to get even. The moment of revenge comes at the trial. She lies and produces false evidence that results in Dmitri's conviction. This is the moment that Katerina has been awaiting. Dishonored and condemned to twenty years' penal servitude, Dmitri now stands as helpless before Katerina as she once stood before him. Even though she is in a position to forgive Dmitri, she finds she cannot. Why? Because it is not hers to forgive. In the desperate effort to place Dmitri in a subservient position, she went too far and injured him much worse than he insulted her. Twenty years in Siberia is not the price one pays for injuring another's pride. Here is the great **irony**. The plan that was meant to repay Dmitri for his insults has boomeranged and put Katerina in an even lower position toward Dmitri than before. On top of that, her conscience bothers her and she has lost her self-respect. It is she, not Dmitri, who must be forgiven.

In short, the sin of pride has led Katerina into a series of acts that culminate in the transgression of one of those inner absolutes which result in the disintegration of the personality. This is how Dostoyevsky illustrates the truth of the saying: "Pride goeth before a fall."

Smerdyakov

"An abyss of shallowness," "a spiritual Quasimodo," "a fragment of a human being" are some of the ways critics describe this person. This man is one of Dostoyevsky's most repellent creations. The illegitimate son of Fyodor and Liza Smerdyaschaya (Stinking Liza), he is what one might expect from the union between the town profligate and the village idiot.

Although affectionately raised by the family servants, he becomes disrespectful and hostile toward them when he learns the circumstances of his birth. He is morbidly sensitive about his parentage and his nickname "Smerdyakov" (Stinker) and sulks for days if someone alludes to it. Furthermore, he resents that his brothers have all the rights and privileges of birth while he is the cook and has nothing. He dislikes Fyodor for treating him as a lackey and denying his legitimacy. To compensate, he affects the manners and dress of the aristocracy. His clothes are expensive, he wears lacquered boots, and spends his money on perfumes, soaps, and pomades. He has also adopted the arrogant mannerisms of the upper classes, particularly in dealing with people of the lower classes. If we add to this pride, jealousy, and wounded vanity it is easy to see what motivates him to crime.

While Fyodor gives Smerdyakov the motivation, Ivan provides the moral sanction for crime. Ivan tells him that since God does not exist, there are no absolutes governing human behavior and men are free to decide for themselves what is good and evil.

Smerdyakov displays considerable intelligence and resourcefulness in arranging Fyodor's death. His original plan calls for manipulating events so that Dmitri will actually commit the murder. First, he persuades Ivan to leave. Knowing his brother's true feelings about his father, this proves to be an easy task. In the day preceding the crime, he whets his master's appetite by falsely telling him that Grushenka has promised to come to him within the next few days. Meanwhile, he tells Dmitri about the money in the envelope, the signals for announcing Grushenka's arrival, and encourages him to believe that she is seriously contemplating his father's offer. On the evening of the crime, Smerdyakov simulates an epileptic seizure to establish his own alibi. But at the last minute, Dmitri finds within himself the strength to resist the murderous impulse and Smerdyakov performs the deed on the spur of the moment. That Dmitri is arrested and prosecuted for the crime is a matter of complete indifference to Smerdyakov. In fact, he thinks that both his father and Dmitri got what they deserved.

In Smerdyakov, Ivan's theories are carried to their ultimate conclusion. Ivan's idea, simply stated, is about morality. He claims that such concepts as right and wrong are arbitrary codes of behavior that have been imposed upon man for the purpose of controlling his unruly nature. Once a person has raised his intelligence to the point where he understands the true nature of morality, he is then free to act according to the dictates of his own will. Ivan expected that man would use his freedom to bring about a better world. Here is the fault in Ivan's reasoning. If a person has no concept of good and evil, how can he be expected to devote himself to good deeds when he does not even understand what the words mean?

Like Svidrigaylov and Stavrogin before him, Smerdyakov is a moral drifter. He lives from day to day following his inclinations without direction. Whether he commits a crime or indulges in some charitable action, he remains emotionally uninvolved. His behavior after the murder shows how freedom from ordinary limitations brings abject boredom. His ennui is not psychological but **metaphysical** in nature. Recognizing no spiritual force outside himself, he holds nothing sacred, believes in nothing, wants nothing. Even the prospect of moving to France or establishing a restaurant in Moscow no longer holds any attraction for him. He finally hangs himself from boredom.

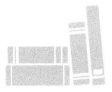

THE BROTHERS KARAMAZOV

ESSAY QUESTIONS AND ANSWERS

· ·

Question: How does everyone in the novel share responsibility for Fyodor's death?

Answer: Everyone in the novel contributes in some way to Fyodor's murder. In a sense, he brings death upon himself in that his depraved way of life repels everyone with whom he comes into contact. He incurs Dmitri's hatred for trying to cheat him of his inheritance, Ivan and Alyosha dislike him because he mistreated their mother, and Smerdyakov kills him partly because Fyodor refuses to recognize him as his legitimate son.

Dmitri is guilty of his father's death because he told everyone of his hatred, threatened in public to kill him, and gave substance to his threats by severely beating him. Then he keeps watch on Fyodor day and night from a hiding place in the garden. Such predictable behavior allows Smerdyakov to lay out detailed plans for the murder and arrange things so that the blame falls on Dmitri.

Ivan shares the greatest portion of guilt for several reasons. First, he desires Fyodor's death from pride. Fyodor, he thinks, is unworthy to be the father of such an intelligent and enlightened individual as himself. He is embarrassed by his profligacy and he is ashamed to be seen with him in public. While in town Ivan develops a relationship with Smerdyakov, reveals his hatred to him, and then provides him with the philosophical justification for murder. Finally, he leaves for Moscow which gives his brother the signal to proceed. The author is careful to point out that Ivan unconsciously knew what he was doing but refused to admit it.

Alyosha is guilty through an act of omission. After the family gathering in Zossima's cell, Zossima warned Alyosha that some **catastrophe** was about to happen and that he should try to prevent it. But Alyosha becomes so preoccupied with the events surrounding the Elder's death that he neglects his duty. Smerdyakov is guilty, of course, not only because he committed the actual deed but also because he failed to understand the ethical basis of Ivan's "everything is lawful," considering it a moral sanction for murder. Katerina is guilty because she gave Dmitri three thousand rubles hoping thereby to obligate him to her. Dmitri's efforts to repay the money help create circumstances which allow Smerdyakov to succeed.

Grushenka shares responsibility because of her spite and desire to revenge herself upon the world. In the beginning she encouraged the attentions of both Fyodor and Dmitri for no other purpose than to laugh at them. By allowing Fyodor to think that she will come to him, he relaxes his guard for a moment on the night of the murder, leans out of the window to look for her and so gives Smerdyakov the chance to strike him from behind.

Finally, the townspeople are accessories to Fyodor's death because they love gossiping about his scandalous life and because none of them attempt to improve the old man.

Everyone in the novel, therefore, participates in Fyodor's murder and shares a common guilt. In this way Dostoyevsky illustrates the truth of Zossima's dictum "all are responsible for all." The author's view of the human condition maintains that man is inextricably involved with everyone else and that the individual can avoid neither the responsibility nor the consequences for such involvement. Smerdyakov kills himself, Ivan almost goes insane, Katerina's reputation is ruined and she may lose Ivan, Dmitri and Grushenka are going into exile, and Alyosha will soon break the law by freeing Dmitri through dishonest means.

Question: What is Dostoyevsky's attitude toward reason?

Answer: Dostoyevsky distrusts rationalism as too far removed from reality. He holds feeling in higher esteem because he believes that only through feeling can we know the totality of any experience. Feeling transcends the limitations imposed by reason. In a letter to his brother Michael October 31, 1838 he wrote: "Nature, the soul, love, and God one recognizes through the heart, and not through reason ... But when our aim is the understanding of love or of nature, we march toward the very citadel of the heart ... Philosophy cannot be regarded as a mere equation where nature is the unknown quantity." There is a similar statement in *Notes from Underground*. The Underground Man claims that man does not consistently act as his reason and advantage dictate because the assumption that man is a rational creature is simply not valid. He rejects reason because it represents only one side of man's being. The explanation for this attitude is not far to seek. He disagrees with certain thinkers who claim the existence of laws governing human behavior much like those governing the physical universe. If such laws exist, man can eventually set up tables of behavior predictive of every human action as he has done for mathematics. But the Underground Man rejects the laws of human nature and says that man is free to create his own law. He maintains that there is no a priori good and evil in the world. Man does not choose what is already determined, rather all human actions are devoid of value until their value is determined at the moment of choice. This way of looking at ethics illustrates the author's belief in man's basic goodness. As long as the individual makes feeling the basis of his ethical behavior, in most cases good will be the result.

BIBLIOGRAPHY

Amend, Victor E. "**Theme** and Form in *The Brothers Karamazov*," *Modern Fiction Studies*, IV (1958), 240-252. Disproves the contention that the sub-themes of the novel (i.e., "The boys") are unessential to the story.

Beebe, Maurice, and Christopher Newton. "Dostoevsky in English: A Selected Checklist of Criticism and Translations," *Modern Fiction Studies*, IV (1958), 271-291. A good source for English works on Dostoyevsky through 1957.

Bohatec, Josef. *Der Imperialismus Gedanke und die Lebens-philosophie Dostojewskjs*. Graz, 1951. An exhaustive study of the author as philosopher.

Berdyaev, Nicholas. *Dostoevsky*, New York, 1957.

Braun, Maximilian. "*The Brothers Karamazov* as an Expository Novel." *Canadian-American Slavic Studies*, 6 (1972), 199-208. Presents evidence that the novel was intended as an "introduction" to a much more important sequel which the author never wrote.

Bursov, Moris. "Dostoyevsky as a Person." *Soviet Literature*, 10 (1971), 152-168. Contains some useful information about Dostoyevsky's personal life. Tries to show how his literary creations are but elaborations of personal experience.

Carr, Edward Hallet, *Dostoevsky (1821-1881): A New Biography*. Boston and New York, 1931. A particularly good treatment of the man and the novelist.

Cox, Roger. "Dostoyevsky's Grand Inquisitor." *Cross Currents*, 17 (1968), 427-444. He shows that the events of the novel prove wrong the Inquisitor's Euclidian view of man.

Curtis, James M. "Spatial Form as the Intrinsic **Genre** of Dostoyevsky's Novesw." *Modern Fiction Studies*, 18 (1972), 135-154. Shows how a study of the novel's form and structure contributes to a fuller understanding of the book's meaning. Structuralist.

Fanger, Donald. "Dostoyevsky Today; Some Recent Critical Studies." *Survey*, XXXVI (1961), 13-19. Analyzes recent trends in Dostoyevsky scholarship.

Friedman, Maurice. *Problematic Rebels; Melville, Dostoyevsky, Kafka, Camus.* University of Chicago Press, 1970.

Gibian, George. "The Grotesque in Dostoyevsky," *Modern Fiction Studies*, IV (1958), 262-270. Discusses the reasons for and the effects of the author's use of the grotesque and the repulsive.

Gregg, Richard. "Apollo Underground: His Master's Still Small Voice." *Russian Review*, 32, pp. 64-67. Society is viewed as a prison, but with the Underground Man trying to get in, not out.

Grossman, Leonid. *Dostoevsky*. Moscow, 1962. Among the best Soviet studies.

Hesse, Hermann. "*The Brothers Karamazov* or The Decline of Europe," in *My Belief: Essays on Life and Art*, ed. Theodore Ziolkowski (New York, 1974), pp.70-85. He predicts the fall of Europe and that the Russian spirit of the Karamazovs will take over as the ideal of the future.

Ivanov, Vyacheslav. *Freedom and the Tragic Life: A Study in Dostoyevsky*, trans. Norman Cameron. New York, 1957. Among the best works on Dostoyevsky. Emphasizes the mythological aspect.

Jackson, Robert L. "Dmitri Karamazov and the Legend." *Slavic and East European Journal*, IX (1966), 257-267. The Grand Inquisitor is wrong and Dmitri's salvation proves it.

Jones, Malcolm. "Dostoyevsky's Conception of the Idea." *Renaissance and Modern Studies*, 3 (1969), 106-131.

Kanzer, Mark. "The Vision of Father Zossima." *American Imago*, VIII (1951), 329-335. Parricide as a Psychological phenomenon. Freudian.

Lavrin, Janko. *Dostoevsky: A Study*. New York, 1947. A brief, incisive analysis of the main novels.

Lukacs, Georg. *Der russische Realismus in der Welt Literatur*. Berlin, 1948. A Marxist interpretation.

Magarschack, David. *Dostoevsky*. New York, 1961. A good, general introduction.

Matlaw, Ralph E. "Thanatos and Eros: Approaches to Dostoevsky's Universe." *Slavic and East European Journal*, IV (1960), 17-24. Explicates the role of death and love in the author's works.

____. "Recurrent **Imagery** in Dostoevsky." *Harvard Slavic Studies*, III (Cambridge, Mass., 1957), 201-225.

Mirsky, D. S. *History of Russian Literature*. New York, 1949. A sober, cool interpretation.

Mochulsky, Konstantin. *Dostoevsky; His Life and Works*. Princeton Univ. Press, 1967. A standard work on the subject. Somewhat unrestrained in its praise.

Oates, Joyce. "The Double Vision of *The Brothers Karamazov.*" *Journal of Aesthetics and Art Criticism*, 27 (1969), 203-213. Focuses on the literariness of the novel.

Pachmuss, Temira. *F. M. Dostoevsky: Dualism and Synthesis of the Human Soul.* Carbondale, Illinois. 1963.

Panichas, George A. "Dostoyevsky and Satanism." *Journal of Religion*, XLV (1966), 12-69. A discussion of the author's concept of evil.

Payne, Robert. *Dostoevsky.* New York, 1961. The best biography available in English.

Rahv, Philip. "The Legend of the Grand Inquisitor." *Partisan Review*, XXI (1054), 249-271. A careful textual analysis of "The Legend" proves that victory belongs to the Grand Inquisitor.

Ramsey, Paul. "No Morality without Immortality: Dostoevsky and the Meaning of Atheism." *Journal of Religion*, XXXVI (1956), 90-108.

_____."God's Grace and Man's Guilt." *Journal of Religion*, XXXI (1951), 21-37. Investigates the **theme** of guilt and redemption.

Rosen, Nathan. "Chaos and Dostoevsky's Women," *Kenyon Review*, XX (1958), 257-277.

_____. "Style and Structure in *The Brothers Karamazov.*" *Russian Literature Triquarterly*, 1 (1971), 352-365. Christ is proved right. Examines the novel on the basis of Dostoyevsky's statement that "the whole novel serves as an answer" to "The Legend" and shows how the Inquisitor's view of man is refuted.

Roodkovsky, Nikita. "Dostoevsky: Seer of Modern Totalitarianism." *Thought*, 47 (1972), 587-598. The author as prophet. "Some of the most characteristic features of the Soviet totalitarian system were seen by Dostoevsky through his knowledge of the radical Russian intelligentsia of his day."

Rozanov, Vasily. *Dostoevsky and The Legend of the Grand Inquisitor*. Cornell Univ. Press: Ithaca, 1972. Among the best analyses of "The Legend."

Rudicina, Alexandra. "Crime and Myth: The Archetypal Pattern of Rebirth in Novels of Dostoevsky," *Publications of the Modern Language Association*, 87 (1973), 1065-1074.

Seduro, Vladimir. *Dostoevsky in Russian Literary Criticism*, 1846-1956. New York: Columbia Univ. Press, 1957.

Simmons, Ernest J. *Dostoevsky: The Making of a Novelist*. London, 1950. A standard work. Very readable.

Simons, John D. "The Nature of Suffering in Schiller and Dostoevsky," *Comparative Literature*, 19 (1967), 160-173.

____."The Myth of Progress in Schiller and Dostoevsky." *Comparative Literature*, 24 (1972), 328-337.

Spilka, Mark. "Human Worth in *The Brothers Karamazov*." *Minnesota Review*, V (1966), 38-49. An examination of the novel's characters establishes the author's concept of human worth which proves the Grand Inquisitor wrong about man.

Steiner, George. *Tolstoy or Dostoevsky; An Essay in the Old Criticism*. New York, 1959. Many good insights, though with a tendency to generalize.

Trilling, Lionel. "Manners, Morals, and the Novel," *The Liberal Imagination*. New York, 1950.

Wasiolek, Edward. *Dostoevsky; the Major Fiction.* Cambridge, Mass., 1964. Probably the best criticism in any language. Penetrating character analysis, psychological techniques sanely used. Emphasizes the author's view of the human condition.

____. "Aut Caesar, aut Nihil: A Study of Dotoevsky's Moral Dialectic," *Publications of the Modern Language Association,* LXXVIII (1963), 89-97.

____.*The Brothers Karamazov and the Critics.* Wadsworth: Belmont, Calif. 1967.

____. ed. and trans. *The Notebooks for The Brothers Karamazov.* Univ. of Chicago Press, 1971.

Wellek, Rene, ed. *Dostoevsky; A Collection of Critical Essays.* Englewood Ciffs, N.J. 1962. The introduction by Wellek discusses virtually every Dostoevsky critic through 1961. Essays by Zenkovsky, Rahv. D.H. Lawrence, and others.

Wilson, Colin. *The Outsider.* (1956). Sees Dostoyevsky's characters as examples of the search for identity.

Yarmolinsky, Avrahm. *Dostoevsky, His Life and Art.* New York, 1957. A good general introduction.

Zenkovsky, V. V. *A History of Russian Philosophy.* New York, 1953. Treats all Dostoyevsky's writings as forming a coherent philosophy.

TOPICS FOR FURTHER RESEARCH AND CRITICISM

Themes *of The Brothers Karamazov*

Dostoyevsky and Social Criticism

The Brothers Karamazov and Modern Society

The Nature of Guilt in *The Brothers Karamazov*

The Nature of Suffering in *The Brothers Karamazov*

Dostoyevsky's Theory of Punishment

Religion and Atheism in *The Brothers Karamazov*

Sensuality as an Alienation Technique

Ivan Karamazov and the Supremacy of Reason

Dostoyevsky's Philosophy of History

Dostoyevsky and the Myth of Progress

TOPICS FOR PAPERS

1. What is true freedom for Dostoyevsky?

2. Compare Alyosha with Prince Myshkin in *The Idiot*.

3. Read *Brave New World* and compare it to the ideas in "The Legend of the Grand Inquisitor."

4. What is the concept of freedom in *Notes from Underground* and "The Legend"?

5. The **theme** of rebellion in Schiller and Dostoyevsky.

6. Compare Kafka's and Dostoyevsky's view of the human condition.

7. What role do the boys play in the novel?

8. Some readers consider Rakitin more repulsive a figure than Fyodor. If this is so, why?

9. In what way does Katerina torture Dmitri with her love?

10. Hatred and love as the novel's unifying principle.

11. What are the different ways in which myth appears in the novel?

12. In what ways are Kolya Krassotkin and Ivan similar?

13. How does the Grand Inquisitor define freedom and happiness?

14. According to the Inquisitor, in what way did Jesus ask too much of mankind?

15. Why does the Grand Inquisitor say that Christianity is a practical impossibility?

COMPARISON WITH OTHER WRITERS

Dostoyevsky's impact on twentieth-century literature is well-nigh incalculable. A comparison of his work with the following selected authors would be particularly worthwhile:

Gerhart Hauptmann

Theodore Dreiser

Marcel Proust

Franz Werfel

Andrei Gide

D.H. Lawrence

George Orwell

Franz Kafka

Thomas Mann

Hermann Hesse

William Faulkner

Aldous Huxley

Albert Camus

Jean Paul Sartre

PRONUNCIATION OF PRINCIPAL CHARACTERS' NAMES

The transliteration of Russian names into English is phonetic. Depending upon the translation, the author's name is spelled Dostoyevsky, Dostoevsky, Dostoievsky, or Dostoievskij. There is no correct English spelling as such. The Russians pronounce it: dus-TOY-evsky.

Middle names in Russian are patronymics, derived from the first name of the person's father. Thus, all the children of one family will bear the same patronymic. The masculine and feminine forms vary slightly.

Alyosha (Alyosha). The youngest and most religious son of Fyodor.

Dmitri (Dmeetree). Fyodor's eldest son. Hotblooded and passionate.

Fetyukovich (Fyetyukovich). Dmitri's lawyer.

Fyodor (Fyodor). The father of the four sons.

Grigory (Grigoree). Family servant.

Grushenka (Grooshenka). The object of Fyodor's and Dmitri's passion.

Ilusha (Eelyusha). Captain Snegiryov's son. Dies of consumption.

Ivan (Eevan). Fyodor's intellectual son.

Katerina Ivanovna (Kahtyereena Eevahnuvna). The woman who wants to marry Dmitri.

Kolya Krassotkin (Koly a Krasotkin). The precocious leader of the schoolboys.

Miusov (Mewsoff.) The superficial liberal.

Rakitin (Rahkeeteen). A novice and unprincipled opportunist at the monastery.

Smerdyakov (Smyerdyakof). Fyodor's illegitimate son.

Snegiryov, Capt. (Snyegeeryof). Father of Ilyusha.

Zossima (Zosseemah). The Elder of the monastery.

CHRONOLOGICAL TABLE OF DOSTOYEVSKY'S MAIN WORKS

1846 *Poor Folk*, *The Double*, "The Landlady", "White Nights".

1858 "Uncle's Dream".

1859 "The Village Stepanchikovo"

1861-62 "The Insulted and Injured", *Notes from the House of the Dead*.

1863 "Winter Notes on Summer Impressions".

1864 *Notes from Underground.*

1865 *Crime and Punishment.*

1866 *The Gambler.*

1868 *The Idiot.*

1870 "The Eternal Husband"

1871-72 The Possessed

1873 "A Gentle Creature", First installments of *The Diary of a Writer.*

1875 *A Raw Youth.*

1880 *The Brothers Karamazov.*

Milton Keynes UK
Ingram Content Group UK Ltd.
UKHW021416210224
438230UK00010B/869